PHILIP JODIDIO

RENZO PIANO BUILDING WORKSHOP

The Poetry of Flight

TASCHEN

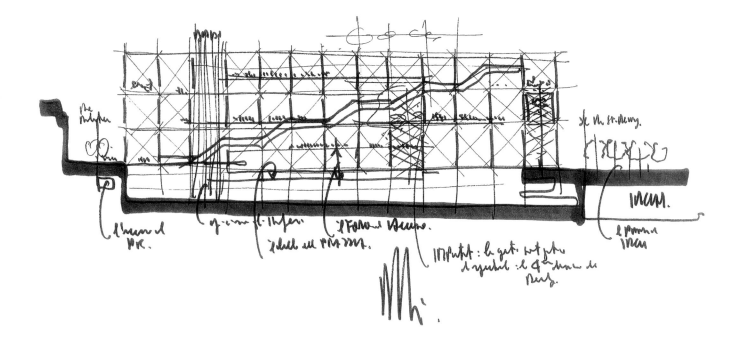

Illustration page 2: Renzo Piano, 2002,
photograph by Gianni Berengo Gardin

Illustration page 4: Centre Georges Pompidou,
Paris, France, 1971–77

© 2016 TASCHEN GmbH
Hohenzollernring 53, D–50672 Köln
www.taschen.com

Editor: Florian Kobler, Berlin
Design: Sense/Net Art Direction, Andy Disl and
Birgit Eichwede, Cologne
Editorial coordination: Inga Hallsson, Berlin
Collaboration: Harriet Graham, Turin
Production: Thomas Grell, Cologne

ISBN 978–3–8365–3646–2
Printed in Slovakia

Contents

Introduction

When Renzo Piano received the 1998 Pritzker Prize, the Jury Citation went a long way to explaining why this Italian-born architect is one of the most significant figures of his profession today. "The array of buildings by Renzo Piano is staggering in scope and comprehensive in the diversity of scale, material, and form. He is truly an architect whose sensibilities represent the widest range of this and earlier centuries—informed by the modern masters that preceded him, reaching back even to the 15th century of Brunelleschi—he has remained true to the concept that the architect must maintain command over the building process from design to built work. Valuing craftsmanship, not just of the hand, but also of the computer, Piano has great sensitivity for his materials, whether using glass, metal, masonry, or wood. Such concepts, values, and sensitivities are not surprising for someone whose father, uncles, and grandfather were all builders."

When Renzo Piano gave his acceptance speech for the Pritzker Prize at the White House, on June 17, 1998, he, too, made reference to his ancestors' profession: "I was born into a family of builders," he said, "and this has given me a special relationship with the art of 'doing.' I always loved going to building sites with my father and seeing things grow from nothing, created by the hand of man. For a child, a building site is magic: today you see a heap of sand and bricks, tomorrow a wall that stands on its own; at the end it has all become a tall, solid building where people can live." And he continued: "Architecture is an art. It uses technique to generate an emotion, and it does so with its own specific language, made up of space, proportions, light, and materials—for an architect, matter is like sound for a musician or words for a poet. There is one theme that is very important for me: lightness (and obviously not in reference only to the physical mass of objects). ... In my architecture, I try to use immaterial elements like transparency, lightness, and the vibration of the light. I believe that they are as much a part of the composition as the shapes and volumes." But where did this idea of lightness, indeed of flight, come from? Was it born of the careful study of architectural history, or did it have more to do with his upbringing?

City of Slate, City of Sails

To explain his thoughts, Piano inevitably refers to Genoa, where he was born. "Genoa," he says with a smile, "is a windy city where I played with the sheets my mother put out to dry and imagined they were sails on some great ship. Genoa is also a heavy city. Paul

Centre Georges Pompidou, Paris, 1971–77
One of the most recognizable features of the
Pompidou Center is its snaking escalator.

Valéry called it 'a city of slate,' but I grew up with the idea of doing the contrary."[1] Citing authors such as Italo Calvino, Renzo Piano makes the leap from these images of his childhood to a more adult vision of lightness. "When you begin to understand lightness," he says, "you discover that it is an attitude of the spirit. Intelligence can be heavy-going or light, and with age one discovers that a light intelligence is much more interesting."

Renzo Piano succeeds in being lighthearted even when it is clear that, for him, architecture is a deadly serious business. It is the balance that he strikes between weight and flight, between light and shadow, that sets him apart. Weight and shadow are part of any building, but Renzo Piano's architecture moves effortlessly toward the light. Bound by gravity and its own purpose, a Piano building nonetheless prepares to take flight at every instant. This is not a flight from responsibility; it is rather a lightness born of the understanding of weight.

Visitors must judge a building when they use it and often critics and architects themselves will speak of "style." Style might be equated with the personality of the creator of a work of architecture, and yet this is an idea firmly rejected by Piano. "Style is like a golden cage that you lock yourself into. Instead of giving myself joyously and freely to each new project, should I instead seek desperately to design a Piano building? One of the great beauties of architecture is that each time it is like life starting all over again. If you are only worried about being recognized you are making a huge mistake. You are being narcissistic and commercially minded. This is a negation of the very spirit of architecture. I don't like the word 'style,' but coherence is definitely something I seek."

Though he is very interested in art, Renzo Piano speaks more readily of artisans when he explains his work. The coherence or professionalism he seeks is bound closely to repeated gestures. "If I have to design a joint, why should I forget that I have done so a hundred times in the past? ... It is the repetition of gestures, like that of the artisan or the pianist, that creates what I call a 'stratification of experience.' What I seek is not

1   Author's interview with Renzo Piano, Paris,
June 5, 2002. Unless indicated otherwise, all
further quotations by Renzo Piano in this text
come from this interview.

Centre Georges Pompidou, Paris, 1971–77
Many visitors to the Center come as much for the view as for the art.

style but a metabolism of experience." Piano's sympathy for the artisan's gesture may well have to do with his own background. His father, Carlo Piano, and his three brothers created the firm Fratelli Piano on the base of their own father's masonry business. They prospered after the war, building houses and factories as well as selling construction materials. Renzo Piano's older brother Ermanno, who studied engineering in Genoa, took over the business in 1965. Following his graduation from Milan Polytechnic Architecture School in 1964, Renzo Piano worked in the family company. Some of his early work, such as the Italian Industry Pavilion at Expo '70 in Osaka, was carried out in collaboration with his brother.

The Architect and the Engineer
After graduation, Piano entered a formative phase that included work in the offices of Louis Kahn in Philadelphia and the Polish engineer Zygmunt Stanislaw Makowski in London, a central figure in the development of space frames in contemporary architecture. Indeed, Renzo Piano has frequently underlined his admiration for engineers such as Pier Luigi Nervi, Jean Prouvé, and Buckminster Fuller, inventor of the geodesic dome, an admiration that has gone far beyond mere curiosity. His own working relationship with men like Peter Rice shows the enrichment he has brought to his architecture by delving deeply into the applied rigor of the engineer. Peter Rice (1935–92) worked on the Sydney Opera House (1960–67) before joining Piano & Rogers on the Pompidou Center project. "Peter," said Piano, "designed structures like a pianist who can play with his eyes shut." It is interesting that he refers both to his own work and to that of Rice by alluding to the art of the pianist. Yet there was no confusion about their respective roles. As Rice wrote: "The architect, like the artist, is motivated by personal considerations, whereas the engineer is essentially seeking to transform the problem into one where the essential properties of structure, material or some other impersonal element are being expressed. This distinction between creation and invention is the key to understanding the difference between the engineer and the

Centre Georges Pompidou
Sculptures by Henri Laurens on the
upper level of the Center.

architect, and how they can both work on the same project but contribute in different ways."[2]

The architect's interest in details explains much of his relationship to the work of engineers, past and present. How does a building hold up, and what elegant, quietly innovative solution can resolve a given construction and design problem? These are the questions that Rice and others such as Tom Barker have answered with Renzo Piano throughout his career. Piano has said: "Knowing how to do things not just with the head, but with the hands as well: this might seem a programmatic and ideological goal. It is not. It is a way of safeguarding creative freedom."[3]

Technically oriented, Piano was also sensitive to the imaginative and optimistic point of view of figures like Peter Cook and Cedric Price (Archigram) whom he frequented when he taught for three years at the Architectural Association in London. If one imagines the work of Archigram, that of Louis Kahn, and also the soaring forms of Nervi or Fuller, one begins to imagine the sources of Renzo Piano's work. Nor is it surprising that he specifically rejected the siren call of postmodernism early in his career.

Learning the Art

Piano's earliest work, beginning in 1965, is often reminiscent of the technologically inspired work of other architects or engineers, although, significantly, he seems almost never to have consciously imitated another designer. Be it in his 1968 IPE Factory in Genoa with its reinforced polyester and steel roof, or his studies for a pavilion at the XIV Milan Triennial (1968), a continuous membrane design, Piano immediately challenged the conventions of architectural form. The Milan pavilion is remarkable because it represents a very early attempt to break out of the strictures of Euclidean geometry in architecture, seeking free forms related to elasticity and movement and in so doing anticipating some contemporary trends by more than 30 years.

It may be interesting to note that, although they did not know each other at the time, Renzo Piano and Peter Rice were already experimenting in related areas. Rice was work-

2 Peter Rice, *An Engineer Imagines*, Artemis, London, 1994.
3 1998 Pritzker Prize brochure.

Centre Georges Pompidou
The Brancusi Atelier seen from the
third level of the Center.

Centre Georges Pompidou
The open platforms of the Center allow
sculptures to be installed—and here provide
a view of the Marais district of Paris.

ing with the Structure 3 group at Ove Arup & Partners in London on a mixture of special
cable and fabric structures, mostly with Frei Otto in Germany. Lightness is often associ-
ated with ephemeral structures, an idea that Renzo Piano espoused from the first. His
1966 Pomezia Factory was designed with polyester panels that could be dismounted to
move the factory to another site, and his IBM Travelling Pavilion (1983–86) took these
ideas to their logical culmination.

Piano's first international commission was the Italian Industry Pavilion for Expo '70
in Osaka. Built with his brother's firm, it was an exercise in lightness and rapidity. The
reinforced polyester and steel structure was assembled in Japan in two months and
drew considerable praise. The forms of this pavilion, though by no means as complex
as those of the Pompidou Center, do bring to mind the later building. Its modular, suspended structure represented a voluntary juncture between industry and architecture,
and Paris was soon to see the results of this experimentation on a much larger scale.

Expo '70 was indeed to have several important consequences for Renzo Piano. One
of those who admired the Italian Industry Pavilion was the architect Richard Rogers.
Even closer to the Pompidou Center in appearance and design, the administrative
building for B&B (Novedrate, Como, 1971–73) was a first collaborative effort with Rogers. Again modular and suspended, the B&B structure also features the visible systems
and bright blue, red, and yellow coloring that was to make a notable appearance in
central Paris shortly thereafter.

A Factory for Culture

For both Renzo Piano, 35 years old, and Richard Rogers, 38, winning the competition
for the Pompidou Center in Paris in 1971 brought almost instant international notori-
ety. After a number of small buildings, Piano was suddenly called on to design 100 000
square meters of space intended to showcase not only art, but also design, performing
arts, and a library. The surprising shapes conceived by Piano and Rogers were to receive
a mixed public reaction at the outset, but a steady flow of 20 000 visitors a day has

marked the Center since its opening. "Beaubourg," says Piano, "was intended to be a joyful urban machine, a creature that might have come from a Jules Verne book, or an unlikely looking ship in dry dock … Beaubourg is a double provocation: a challenge to academics, but also a parody of the technological imagery of our time. To see it as high-tech is a misunderstanding," he concludes.

Another significant participant in the Paris project was Peter Rice, who describes it in different terms: "It was a large, loose-fit frame where anything could happen. At its core was the belief, which had been identified in the brief, that culture should not be elitist, that culture should be like any other form of information: open to all in a friendly, classless environment."[4] Indeed, almost without knowing it, Renzo Piano, by winning the Pompidou competition, took a great step to defining not a style, but rather the coherence that he speaks of so convincingly today. Was the Pompidou Center a "parody of the technological imagery of our time," or was it aesthetically speaking a product of the 1960s, and therefore out of date from the first? With its flexibility and technical orientation, even in the details of its construction, the Center does bring together the fruits of industry and the general public in an edifice destined to break the elitist view of culture. The National Museum of Modern Art housed in the Palais de Tokyo, a new Center for Industrial Design (CCI), an experimental music facility (IRCAM) headed by Pierre Boulez, and a large library were also part of the brief.

Engineering, and indeed Peter Rice, also played a role in a second museum structure designed by Renzo Piano, the Menil Collection (Houston, Texas, 1981–87). In the period of nine years between the opening of the first structure and that of the second, Renzo Piano clearly moved toward a more mature approach to architecture. Still fascinated by details and materials, he no longer felt the need to display the technical "guts" of a building. As he says: "Paradoxically, the Menil Collection, with its great serenity, its calm, and its understatement, is far more 'modern,' scientifically speaking, than Beaubourg. The technological appearance of Beaubourg is parody. The technology used for the Menil Collection is even more advanced (in its structures, materials, systems of climate control), but it is not flaunted." Then, too, the project in Texas was

Menil Collection, Houston, Texas, 1981–87
Renzo Piano (standing) with the engineers Peter Rice and Tom Barker.

4   Peter Rice, *An Engineer Imagines*, Artemis, London, 1994.

Menil Collection, Houston, Texas, 1981–87
The sunshades of the building were partially inspired by the forms of nature.

very different in both scale and intentions. Rather than a state bureaucracy, the client—Dominique de Menil—in this instance was an individual. She insisted on the necessity of using as much natural light as possible and this led the architect to look at innovative systems for the control and utilization of the bright Texas sun.

Sometimes cited as Piano's best building, the Menil Collection is modest in appearance. Its walls are simple, and so, in appearance, is the roof. But Piano and Rice had carefully studied the ceiling and resolved the light problem with a modular leaflike system. Their solution called on unusual materials. As Rice wrote: "Ferro-cement and ductile iron were two of these materials. In combining them we sought to weave together the porcelain-like fragility of the ductile iron with the soft, grainy texture of the ferro-cement into a continuous melded whole."[5] With Menil, Piano's search for lightness and transparency reached new heights. He succeeded in subordinating the technical aspects of the building to its overall purpose, thus moving closer to a work of pure architecture, as opposed to an engineering *tour de force*.

The Transparent and the Opaque

In a way, Piano's goal came to be the consistent use of the best available technology in the least obtrusive way possible. What visitors noted most about his IBM Travelling Pavilion (1983–86), was not so much the building but what it displayed, and the views through its walls. Again, it was Peter Rice who worked behind the scenes to bring the architect's ideas to life. "The concept," explains Rice, "was to have a series of polycarbonate pyramids which, together with timber inner and outer members, would act as a semicircular arch spanning 12 meters and creating an internal space which would, when placed in a suitable natural setting, give the sense of being with nature." Designed to be moved from one location to another on specially designed trucks, the IBM Pavilion was both light and intentionally ephemeral. By adding transparency (coupled with appropriate sun shading) to the equation, Piano proved that far from being repetitive or superficial, contemporary architecture could invent new solutions to specific problems.

In 1983, Renzo Piano took on a far heavier piece of architecture: the Lingotto Automobile Factory in Turin, praised by Le Corbusier in his 1923 manifesto *Vers une architecture*. Built between 1917 and 1920 by the engineer Giacomo Mattè Trucco, Lingotto was notable for its considerable size, and also for its rooftop car test track. Piano decided to keep its original form, while progressively adding new facilities. The first of these was a concert hall that he created by digging 14 meters into the inner courtyard (1990–94). The second was the Heliport and Bubble Panoramic Meeting Room (1992–95) that he perched on top of the structure. A more recent addition is the so-called Pinacoteca, designed to house the Agnelli art collection. Despite the apparent weight of the rooftop structure, it, too, seems poised to take off like the earlier helipad. When modernism was at its postwar height, dealing with as cumbersome a structure as Lingotto could only have inspired architects with a desire to raze it to the ground and start anew. Clearly sensitive to industrial heritage and personally interested in factory design, Renzo Piano brought an incremental approach to Lingotto, based on preserving its initial profile and linked to the desires of the client (Fiat), but his additions also ran counter to many modernist assumptions. When asked about the very heaviness of Lingotto, and the significance of his own interventions there, Piano replies: "It is a heavy building, but one that can still go forward. The Pinacoteca is symbolically and

5   Peter Rice, *An Engineer Imagines*, Artemis, London, 1994.

IBM Travelling Pavilion, 1983–86
Photographed here near the Castel Sant'Angelo in Rome.

physically heavy ... Nonetheless it floats too, it flies above Lingotto. This is certainly not just a question of weight though, it is one of movement. One might speak of metamorphosis, of the capacity of something to transform itself."

The Call of the Pacific

Far from his native country, Piano took another major step toward the international recognition he has attained today when he won the prestigious competition for the Kansai International Airport Terminal (Osaka, Japan, 1988–94). Set on an artificial island located in the Bay of Osaka, the structure had to deal with the potential for earthquakes and the natural settling of the island. Although the land has dropped more than experts predicted since the opening of the facility, the adjustable system of hydraulic pistons has proven equal to the challenge. Then too, set as close as Kobe to the epicenter of the so-called Hanshin Earthquake of 1995, Kansai Airport suffered no damage.

As is often the case, Renzo Piano describes his own buildings with a clarity that fully demonstrates the fundamental logic of his work. "With Tom Barker, a mechanical engineer with Ove Arup & Partners," he says, speaking about Kansai Airport, "we investigated streams of air, from which the form of the terminal's roof would emerge. In cross section, the roof is an irregular arch (in reality a series of arches of different radii), given this shape to channel air from the passenger side of the terminal to the runway side without the need for closed ducts. Baffles left open to view guide the airflow along the ceiling and reflect the light coming from above. We were creating an aerodynamic ceiling, concerned not with the flow of air outside, but inside. Kansai is a precision instrument, a child of mathematics and technology. It forms a strong and recognizable landmark; it has a clear and simple shape that declares itself without hesitation. It is a structure with undulating, asymmetrical lines. It spreads over the island like a glider—a missing link between ground and airplane. In the absence of other constraints, the only factor that has shaped its volumes is the space taken up by the aircraft and their maneuvering. The planes determine form, function, and extension.

Lingotto Automobile Factory, Turin, 1983–2003
The original test track on the roof of the factory was kept intact.

Lingotto Automobile Factory, Turin, 1983–2003
The Meridien Hotel was added to the complex in 2003.

They are the true masters of the island. We have paid homage to these local divinities with a departure area that has 42 passenger-loading bridges and extends for 1700 meters, and is capable of handling 100 000 passengers a day. Kansai is one of the largest buildings ever built, three Lingottos in a row."[6]

If Renzo Piano's singular lack of "style" was not yet apparent in his production up to the early 1990s, his Jean-Marie Tjibaou Cultural Center (Nouméa, New Caledonia, 1991–98) made it abundantly clear. Here, he faced the challenge of building a cultural center dedicated to the Kanak civilization. He studied local culture before proposing a "village" made up of 10 spaces of different sizes and functions. For the most part approximately 28 meters in height, the structures face a main "street" on one side, and expose their rounded wooden backs to sea winds. Making maximum use of natural ventilation, Piano ventured with the Tjibaou Center into the area of "sustainable" architecture. Much like "sustainable" development, this concept has many variants, but there is an implied respect for nature that Renzo Piano surely does not reject. As he said: "Nature is not made with the measure of man in mind. I personally love the sea, but despite 45 years of sailing, I still fear and respect it. If man didn't protect himself from nature, nature would see him off ... Man feels more comfortable constructing this new nature. It nevertheless happens that original nature is so powerful that only by interpreting it, only by using its own norms, can another be created."[7]

Renzo Piano's encounter with the Pacific, be it in Nouméa or in Japan, seems to have been significant in his development as an architect. He says: "I was 50 years old when I discovered the culture of the Pacific. It is a culture of lightness and of the ephemeral. Although I grew up in Europe, I feel much closer to the Pacific, where lightness, or the wind, is much more durable than stone. This is due to the ritual repetition of gestures from generation to generation. In Japan, there is no doubt that the culture of lightness and of the ephemeral is much more stable than the solidity of any stone. In California it is the tradition of Neutra and Eames, just as in Australia, architecture is often linked to the idea of the ephemeral."

6 1998 Pritzker Prize brochure.
7 Renzo Piano, *Sustainable Architecture*, Editorial Gustavo Gili, Barcelona, 1998.

Urban Man

In one of a series of large-scale urban projects he has undertaken since the mid-1990s, Renzo Piano has demonstrated his consciousness of the importance of scale and location. In 1996 he began work on one of the largest projects of his career, the reconstruction of a section of Potsdamer Platz (Berlin, Germany, 1992–2000). As he says: "Cities are beautiful because they are created slowly; they are made by time. A city is born from a tangle of monuments and infrastructures, culture and market, national history and everyday stories. It takes 500 years to create a city, and 50 to create a neighborhood. We have been asked to reconstruct a large chunk of Berlin in the space of five years." The most visible element of his contribution is the 45000-square-meter Debis Headquarters, with its 21-story tower clad in a double skin of glass, obviating the need for excessive air conditioning or heating.

On a much smaller scale, Renzo Piano recently completed the Maison Hermès in Tokyo (1998–2001). This surprising glass-block structure is located in the heart of Ginza, one of the most vibrant and active commercial areas of the Japanese capital. As Piano says: "Architecture is capable of metamorphosis when it is based on the play and vibration of light. The Maison Hermès is a building that is made of nothing, and yet it changes 1000 times a day. The idea of lightness or flight is too simple to describe this. It is about the marvelous tension that exists between durability and the transient. The ephemeral is beauty in its purest state." Piano is of course being modest when he says the Maison Hermès is "made of nothing." The glass-block design required special manufacturing by Vetroarredo in Florence to meet stringent Japanese fire and earthquake standards. Whatever the weather conditions, the building shimmers in daylight and glows from within at night, becoming the "magic lantern" referred to by the architect.

Halfway around the world from Tokyo, Renzo Piano has also made a substantial mark in Manhattan. Few really well-known international architects ever get the opportunity to build in New York, and Piano has been selected for three projects. The 52-story New York Times Building is intended to be as open and transparent as possible, sym-

Parco della Musica Auditorium, Rome, 1994–2002
The 1200-seat concert hall is essentially rectangular with a rounded exterior shell.

**The Whitney Museum of American Art,
New York, New York, 2007–2015**
A view of the rooftop terraces of the
museum that allow visitors to view
the neighborhood and also serve for the
outdoor exhibition of sculptures.

bolizing the relationship of the newspaper to the city. Talking about the building Piano
says: "I like fighting gravity. Magic is essential in architecture. Working in Manhattan, I
love the idea that we accept the clear and simple geometry of a building. We accept that
logic. But complexity comes from texture, from vibration, from the metamorphic capacity of the building to transform, to change, to breathe ... The building is actually very
simple. But the complexity comes from the skin, the surface of the building actually
vibrating, working with the weather."[8] Piano's second major project in Manhattan is
equally prestigious if somewhat less visible—the Morgan Library on Madison Avenue—where, significantly, the better part of his design is located underground. In this
case, he insists neither on the concepts of lightness nor of the ephemeral, though the
glass-covered area is anything but heavy. "There are buildings like the Morgan Library
that are meant to last—and why not?—for a thousand years. That is how we worked.
Why dig deep into the bedrock of New York? To safeguard the rare books of the
Morgan ... forever."

Piano's third major project in Manhattan concerns the Whitney Museum of American Art, long located in Marcel Breuer's 1966 landmark building on Madison Avenue.
After years of exploring possible expansion of the museum in the area of its site, first
with Michael Graves and then with Rem Koolhaas, in 2008, the Whitney commissioned
Renzo Piano to create an entirely new building in the city's Meatpacking District. Located between Washington and Gansevoort Streets near the renovated High Line, the
new structure opened in 2015. The nine-story, 20000-square-meter building offers
4645 square meters of interior gallery space, and a further 1208 square meters outside
for sculptures. Asymmetrical and cantilevered, creating a public plaza at ground level,
the structure seeks to "respond to the industrial character of neighboring buildings"
and overlooks the Hudson River to the west and the High Line closer by.

Berlin, Tokyo, and New York are not the only major cities where Renzo Piano has
worked recently or has new projects underway. In Sydney, within view of Jørn Utzon's
Opera House, he completed the Aurora Place towers in 2000, and in London he took

8 Renzo Piano, interview by Robert Ivy,
Architectural Record, October 2001, http:
//archrecord.construction.com/people
/interviews/archives/0110piano.asp

on a more controversial effort to rise to the skies. His 306-meter-tall London Bridge Tower (called The Shard; 2000–12) is the tallest office building in the European Union. His own statement sets out his vision for this structure. "I see the tower like a vertical little town for about 10 000 people to work in and enjoy and for hundreds of thousands more to commute to and from. This is why we have included shops, museums, offices, restaurants, and residential spaces within its 72 floors. The shape of the tower is generous at the bottom without arrogantly touching the ground, and narrow at the top, disappearing in the air like a 16th-century pinnacle or the mast top of a very tall ship … Architecture is about telling stories and expressing visions, and memory is part of it. Our memory is permeated by history. That is why this design alludes to spires."

Jean-Marie Tjibaou Cultural Center, Nouméa, New Caledonia, 1991–98
Inspired by local hut design, the structures rise to a maximum height of 28 meters.

Roots in the Earth, Head in the Stars
One wonders how Renzo Piano retains his warmth and courtesy in the midst of his world-girdling list of projects. One wonders, too, how he approaches new work without ceding to the kind of repetitive "style" that he obviously rejects. "Things have changed a lot for me," he admits. "I used to be quite bad at 'listening' to sites. When you are young, your system of registering things is not yet fully formed. And I had such a joy in manipulating materials.... With age, we begin to understand some things better, don't we? I never get involved in a project without having spent some time on the site … listening. I spend a day or two doing small sketches on the site. They are like a form of shorthand for me; I use them in order to be able to discuss certain points with my staff.... Forget about style, there is professionalism. We usually define the basic outlines of a project quickly at the office, but afterwards there is a great deal of thinking and refining that is done. Architecture is slow work. Having a good idea at the outset is one thing. Keeping it right up to the end is another," he concludes.

Renzo Piano is an optimist, but a lucid one. How often does he balance one quest with its opposite, juxtaposing a form deeply rooted in the earth with the metaphor of flight, at Kansai Airport for example. It is also Piano's deep respect for the mechanics

of architecture, and for the talents of great engineers that permits him to give something more to his architecture than an attractive façade. This is a man who lives and breathes architecture. Yet this is also a man who designs his own sailboats and leaves his office and work far behind every year to be on the sea. Technology can certainly be cold, but in Piano's hands, working with men like Peter Rice, it is bent to a will. Materials ranging from glass blocks to ceramic panels or Puglia sandstone in the case of the Padre Pio Church are fashioned not as though they came off an assembly line, but rather as though the hand of the architect had individually touched them. An optimist, a modern humanist, a man smitten with love for his art, for his profession—these are all descriptions that fit Renzo Piano. In a profession where each element can weigh tons, Renzo Piano has succeeded in retaining the lightness of his youth, an enthusiasm and an openness that has the world beating a path to his door. Rather than a style, his clients have sought an approach that varies in accordance with each site, each function. Renzo Piano is a master of the mechanics of lightness. He knows that architecture is bound to the earth, but it is in the equilibrium of tension between earth and sky that he has found his place. The 250-ton Pinacoteca hovers on the roof of Lingotto, ready to take to the air. The wind fills the sails of Piano's boat *Kirribilli* and there, finally, movement is his.

1971–1977 ▶ Centre Georges Pompidou

Paris, France

Opposite page
The main façade with its snakelike escalators.

Inside the glass-clad escalators that rise to the top of the building.

Below
A section drawing shows the large scale of the structure as compared to neighboring buildings.

The Pompidou Center is in many ways a seminal structure, not only in the career of Renzo Piano, but also for the architecture of its time. "We were young and it was very much an 'in your face' kind of building," said Piano 20 years later. He may have almost regretted the overtly industrial appearance of the building that has tended to obscure its actual functions. Intended as a showcase of modern French culture in the spirit of President Pompidou, who also facilitated the growth of such urban experiments as the "Front de Seine," the Paris facility was a kind of a giant offspring of Malraux's "maison de la culture" concept. From the first, it embraced various disciplines and forms of expression, ranging from a library to the National Museum of Modern Art. Significantly, the engineer Jean Prouvé was a member of the jury that selected the young team of Renzo Piano and Richard Rogers. Prouvé's own Maison du Peuple in Clichy (1939) has been cited as a precursor of the concept of spatial flexibility so important to the Pompidou project. It was in a way the fulfillment of many 20th-century technological fantasies like those of Buckminster Fuller, but here, with the brilliant assistance of the engineers Peter Rice and Tom Barker, the dream took very real form. Six stories high, with a 48-meter clear span, the Center stands out near the old Marais district of Paris as an ode to technically oriented architecture, with its web of tubular ducts on the east façade and the signature glass escalator, inching up the 166-meter-wide west face. Piano's office sums things up in another way. They say that "Beaubourg," as the Center is more commonly known, was "a double provocation: a challenge to academics but also a parody of the technological imagery of our time." The Pompidou Center, they conclude, "is a 'celibate machine' in which the flaunting of brightly colored metal and tubing serves an urban, symbolic, and expressive function, not a technical one." The

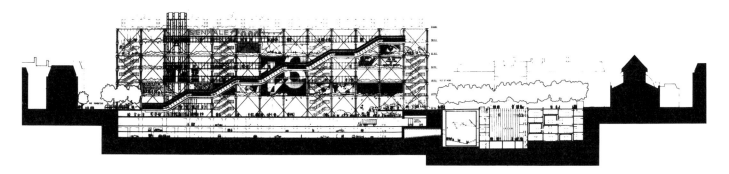

An aerial view confirms the factorylike
impression given by the architecture.

Opposite page top
**The Forum space opening on the
main entry level of the Center.**

Opposite page bottom
**At night, the Center glows from within,
revealing the activity that continues every
day until closing time.**

original Center included the underground facilities of the IRCAM, a contemporary
music complex founded by Pierre Boulez. In 1988–90, Piano added a new, above-
ground structure for the IRCAM, just across the street from the Pompidou Center. Its
composite brick façade clearly announces that by that time the architect had set aside
the Archigram style complexity that characterized the main building. Another small
addition to the Center, the Brancusi Atelier, was added in the early 1990s. Brancusi left
numerous sculptures to the French government on the condition that they remain in
his atelier. The officials of the Center and Piano approached this condition with a
unique combination of modern architecture and a faithful reconstruction of the original studio on the plateau in front of Beaubourg. Coming back to the Pompidou Center
to oversee its renovation in the late 1990s, Piano cleared the structure of the overly
fussy additions brought to the interiors by other designers and gave it back a good
measure of the transparency and openness with which it had been designed. Significantly, it could also be said that his renovation calmed the discordant assemblage of
mechanical forms that had characterized the galleries and other interior public spaces
from 1977 on.

1981–1987 ‣ Menil Collection

Houston, Texas, USA

Opposite page
The curving sunscreens of the building do not seem to be in contradiction with the forms of a tree.

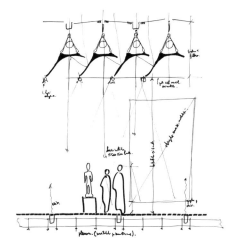

A sketch by Piano shows the scale of visitors vis-à-vis the gallery height and the screens.

Below
The basic form of the structure is purely geometric, but the sunscreen and the light columns give it an airy openness.

It was in 1981 that Dominique de Menil approached Renzo Piano about building a museum for her family's collections of Surrealist and African art in Houston. The design of this structure, calling on natural lighting to the greatest extent possible, seems to be at a great distance from the visibly technological complexity of the Pompidou Center. Conceived 10 years after the Paris building, it is visibly a work of maturity. Working once again with the engineers from Ove Arup & Partners, Piano carefully studied the incidence of light within the exhibition galleries, particularly important in this part of the United States where harsh sun is the rule. It was Dominique de Menil who insisted that the works be visible in the best natural lighting conditions obtainable. The ground-floor exhibitions are complemented by a rooftop "Treasure House" open on appointment and designed in a denser, storage-oriented mode for some 10 000 works of art. The system of ferro-cement and cast ductile iron "leaves" devised for the control of interior lighting extends beyond the walls of the museum to cover pedestrian passageways running alongside. The history of the Menil family's collecting and commitment to modern art is edifying. Having begun to collect art under the influence of Marie-Alain Couturier, the Dominican friar who was largely responsible for Le Corbusier's work at La Tourette and Ronchamp, they also came to appreciate architecture. Their Houston home was built by Philip Johnson in 1948–49, and they organized the first one-man museum show of the work of Max Ernst in the United States in 1952. Beginning in 1964, they worked on the famous Rothko Chapel. Designed by Philip Johnson, it was dedicated in 1971. Renzo Piano succeeded in giving built form to their

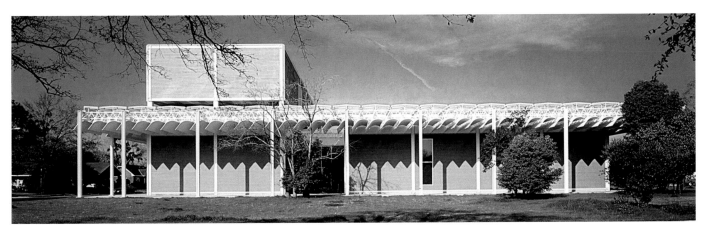

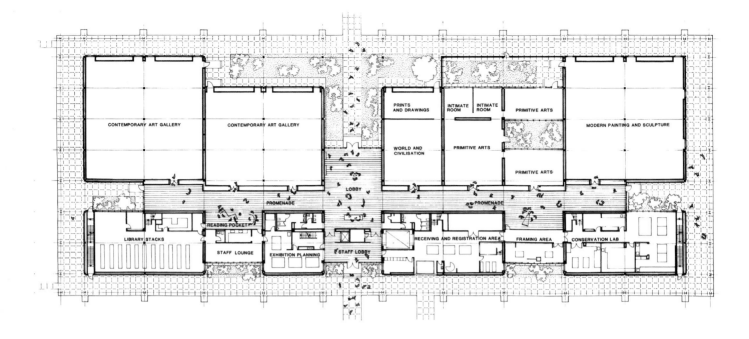

Generous ceiling height and ample natural light allow works to be seen well.

Above
The final version of the ground floor plan with opaque galleries in the lower part, and brighter ones in the upper section.

family tradition of openness and deep interest in the arts and architecture with his design. Dignified and calm, fitting in well with the environment of small wooden houses, the Menil Collection is one of the first real masterpieces of Renzo Piano's career. Piano added a second structure to the Menil Collection. The Cy Twombly Annex (1992–95) is located across Branard Street from the original structure. A square grid with eight rooms, one of which has a double volume, is formed with concrete block walls and a light roof designed to bring ample daylight into the exhibition areas. Piano describes this form as a "butterfly alighting on a firm surface."

Opposite page top
The collection offers a surprising contrast between primitive art and modern pieces.

Opposite page bottom
African art is seen against the backdrop of an enclosed garden.

1985–2001 ▸ Redevelopment of the Old Harbor of Genoa

Genoa, Italy

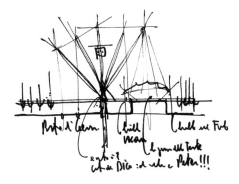

Inspired by harbor cranes, Piano's elevator is seen in his sketch.

Opposite page
Both sails and cranes evoke the atmosphere of the port of Genoa.

Below
A broader view of the harbor installation by Renzo Piano.

The city of Genoa decided late in the 1980s to organize an international exhibition to commemorate the 500th anniversary of the discovery of America by Christopher Columbus. The site selected for the event was part of the old port of Genoa (wharves dating from the 17th to the 20th century), which permitted both the renovation of a historic area of the city and the construction of new, permanent facilities. The project was also to create a new link between Genoa's historic center (near the port) and the sea. In practical terms, the project entailed restoring the old buildings along the port, such as the three-story, 400-meter-long Cotton Warehouse, to provide various facilities, including a library and auditorium. Great care was taken to ensure that these renovations did not betray the original spirit of the district. New buildings, such as an aquarium and a naval derrick—a crane symbolizing the new port, were built, with an equal attention to harmonizing with the spirit of the port. Extending the area's short streets to the waterfront created the port's link to the city: Via del Mare, one of the main thoroughfares of the historic district, was extended along a breakwater near the aquarium, leading to the center of the port. More than the execution of a construction or renovation plan, the project was intended to reclaim something of the port's glorious past. That wager seems to have been won since this part of the city has taken on a life of its own, both night and day.

1983–2003 ▸ Lingotto Factory Conversion

Turin, Italy

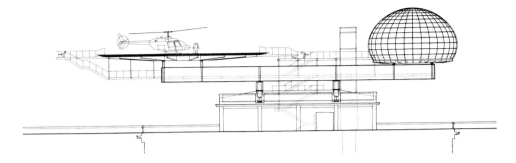

Inside the "Bolla" meeting room on top of the Lingotto Factory.

Top
An elevation drawing of the added structure in position on the factory.

Opposite page top
Piano dubbed this addition for the Agnelli art collection the "flying bank vault."

Opposite page bottom
The exhibition gallery is perched on top of the old factory structure.

The rehabilitation of the Lingotto Factory, a symbol of industrial Turin, is a project that Renzo Piano has been working on since the early 1980s. Built between 1917 and 1920 by the engineer Giacomo Mattè Trucco, Lingotto was praised by Le Corbusier in his 1923 manifesto *Vers une architecture*. From the first, Renzo Piano decided with the client Fiat to retain the fundamental characteristics of the original building. Further, it was decided that the renovation would be a phased project, with each new addition being completed whether or not other elements were ready. Technology of various types was considered the leitmotif of the Lingotto renovation. As Piano wrote: "Once completed, the Lingotto will be a genuine machine, capable of interacting with the climate and linking up to all the communication systems in existence."

Between 1992 and 1995, Renzo Piano added the Heliport and Bubble Panoramic Meeting Room to the former factory. With a capacity of 24 people, the Bubble offers an extensive view of Turin. The addition of the cantilevered helicopter landing pad and the futuristic double-skinned glass dome was a clear sign that Lingotto was being brought into the present. The Bubble appears to float above Lingotto, and the attached helipad reinforces the idea of architecture taking flight. Between 1990 and 1994, a Concert Hall was added to the old factory. The structural work on the heliport, Bubble, and concert hall was finally carried out by Fiat Engineering. In 2002, Renzo Piano added the Giovanni and Marella Agnelli Art Gallery to Lingotto. As his grandson Lapo Elkann said, speaking of Giovanni Agnelli on the occasion of the opening: "He never concealed his ambition: to shift the center of gravity in Turin in this direction, transforming a former factory into a new center, a new magnet for the future development of this city." As early as 1961, Agnelli had asked the architect Carlo Scarpa to design a museum at Villar Perosa, but Scarpa died in 1978 and that project was never carried out. Speaking himself of this project, Giovanni Agnelli says: "Those who come to visit Lingotto will see an area of the outskirts of Turin—between the Alps and the hill on which the city stands—that I have always loved. One of Renzo Piano's special gifts as an architect is that his designs seem to inject new life into the area around a new building [...] the entire place becomes a sort of resonance chamber for the building under construction. The houses, the urban fabric, the metropolis itself become a sort of network, at the center of which the traveler finds a moment of aesthetic repose and reflection." The Pinacoteca, like the Bubble, appears to hover above Lingotto near the edge of its famous test track, its flat roof and ship-like body seemingly poised to fly higher still.

1988–1994 ▸ Kansai International Airport Terminal

Osaka, Japan

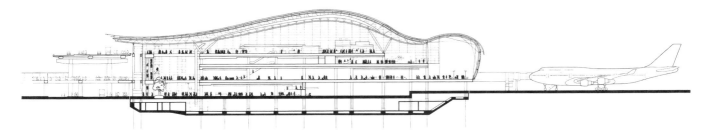

A section drawing shows the curving roof and different levels of the terminal building.

Opposite page
An aerial view of the main terminal.

Below left
Inside the spacious passenger area of the terminal.

Below right
The long, low curvature of the building is visible in this image.

One of the largest architectural and engineering undertakings of the late 20th century, Kansai International Airport was built on a 511-hectare artificial island located in the Bay of Osaka. Piano was selected from a prestigious field in an international competition in 1988. The unusual curved shape of the 1.7-kilometer-long main terminal building is related to air traffic control's need to maintain visual contact with taxiing aircraft at all times. Piano used this formal constraint to the benefit of his design, making reference to works of art such as Brancusi's *Bird in Space*, and aircraft or gliders. It will not escape visitors that the undulating roof also recalls wings for this island airport. The curve of the terminal was, in fact, conceived as a small section of an imaginary 32.8-kilometer-diameter torus, whose main volume would be underground. With its 83-meter-long arches on the upper floor, the terminal offers a real feeling of freedom to travelers. It should be noted that the construction of such a large building on an artificial island posed many technical problems, solved in good part with the assistance of Ove Arup & Partners and Nikken Sekkei, using a system of hydraulic joints designed to compensate for the predicted settling of the landfill. Although from some angles its visible structure may recall the design of the Pompidou Center, Kansai Airport has a flowing ease in its design that was certainly born of Piano's experience. Simply put, the traveler finds his way easily in this airport and, even more important, feels comfortable at all times. Seen from the air, the 82 000 stainless-steel panels covering the 90 000-square-meter roof often shine in the sun, offering a more congenial image than almost any other modern airport in the world. The scale of Kansai International Airport is such that it coincidentally gave rise to a series of other projects, such as Tadao Ando's Awaji-Yumebutai complex built on the nearby island of Awaji on the site deeply scarred by the extraction of landfill for the airport.

1989–1991 ▸ Renzo Piano Building Workshop

Punta Nave (Genoa), Italy

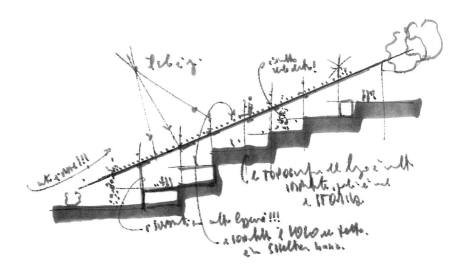

The roof of the structure seems to flow directly into the sea.

Top right
A sketch by Piano shows the stepped design and its exposure to the sun.

Opposite page
Viewed from above, the building is to the right in this image.

Initially linked to a study carried out with UNESCO on "Mediterranean natural structures," the Renzo Piano Building Workshop (RPBW) offices are laid out in an unusual configuration on a slope to the west of Genoa facing the sea. The stepped design recalls neighboring terraces that cascade down toward the shore. An eight-person funicular serves the facility. Conceived like a greenhouse because of the need to study plant species, the structure is designed with a laminated wood frame roof set on thin metal columns. Double glazing with an intermediary layer of air helps to keep heat gain as low as possible, while admitting a maximum amount of natural light to the work areas and offering views toward the sea. Exterior mounted slat shades reduce the penetration of direct sunlight into the workspaces. Aside from the stone and earth wall on the mountainside, the other walls of the structure are also made of glass. According to Renzo Piano, this atelier is made of "space, sun, and nature." Despite his frequent use of technological means, the architect carries his passion for lightness over into the conception of simple and elegant designs such as that of this structure. Making no attempt to carve into the hillside, he prefers to adapt architecture to its site, and to make the interior fully permeable to natural surroundings. In this type of work, Renzo Piano is closer to so-called green architects than he is to any "high-tech" designer.

Renzo Piano at his desk in
the Punta Nave offices.

Below
An overall plan of the Punta Nave building.

Opposite page top
A section drawing shows the interior
spaces and the continuous roof.

Opposite page bottom
The interior is entirely open to
its natural setting.

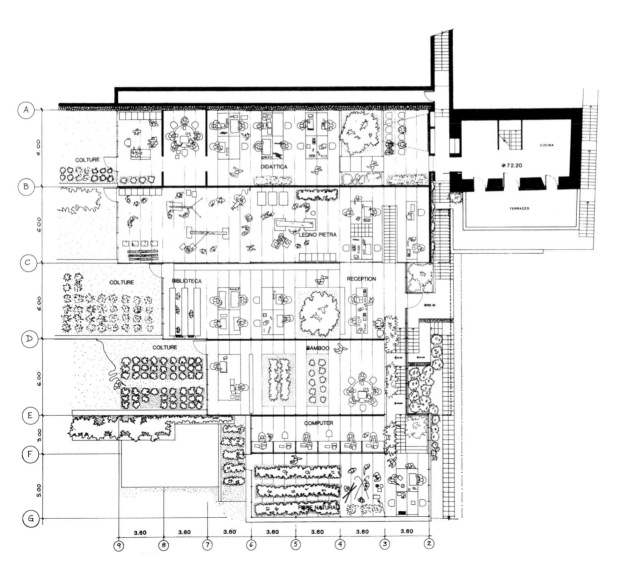

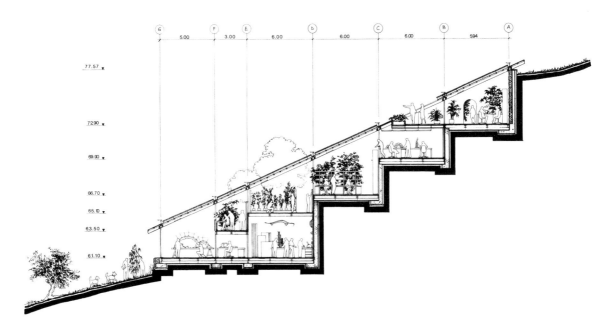

1991–2001 ▸ Banca Popolare di Lodi

Lodi, Italy

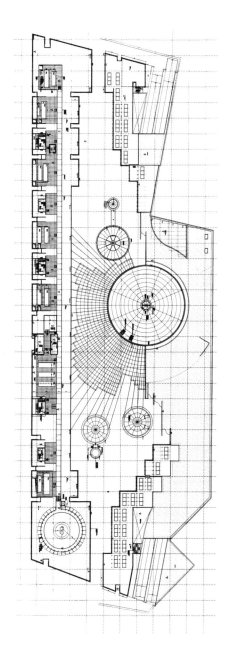

In this project, for one of the largest banks in the Lombardy region of Italy, Renzo Piano proposed an approachable, friendly design, conducive to vegetation and open to pedestrian traffic. The client wished in any case to avoid the fortresslike structures of so many banks. In terms of the overall design, Piano has chosen to make use of cylindrical structures of varying height clad in terra-cotta whose forms and colors evoke a nearby medieval castle and the silos of farmsteads frequently seen in the region. Set on the site of a former dairy farm in the midst of an industrial zone where the Polenghi Lombardo factory was located, the bank is nonetheless at the intersection of two of Lodi's major arteries, close to the train station and the downtown area. Various openings punctuate the large succession of rectangular blocks on the west façade, giving access to a large square inside, covered by a light glass-and-steel cable structure that serves as the meeting place for pedestrians. It is this square that leads to the bank's offices and to an 800-seat auditorium. Retail outlets and other offices have also opened in the complex and the constant movement of pedestrians makes the bank a center for the life of the community.

The plan above shows the entire facility, with the round auditorium in the center.

Right
The interior of the auditorium.

Opposite page
Exterior view with the radiating "spider web" pattern of the canopy.

1991–1998 ▸ Jean-Marie Tjibaou Cultural Center

Nouméa, New Caledonia

Opposite page
A traditional hut being built near the Center.

Below
The independence leader Jean-Marie Tjibaou for whom the Center was named.

Below right
Though he uses wood for interiors, Piano still creates modern, light spaces.

Few architects have built in such far-flung locations as Renzo Piano. Even by his standards though, New Caledonia in Melanesia is a bit off the beaten track. Subsequent to the significant difficulties encountered with the population of New Caledonia by the French government in the late 1980s, it was decided to build a Kanak Cultural Center near the capital of Nouméa. Taking his clue from the disposition of local villages, Piano conceived this Center, set on a narrow peninsula, as a series of wooden pavilions. On the side facing a lagoon with strong dominant winds, the architect erected a series of curving wooden-walled structures ranging from nine to 28 meters in height. While a double-skinned design makes these façades sufficiently resistant even during tropical storms, they are also designed to admit natural light and breeze while encouraging the expulsion of hotter air through a natural "chimney" effect. There are three functional "villages" in the complex. The first contains the public areas and exhibition spaces, the second the auditorium, médiathèque, and meeting rooms, and the third the administrative and teaching areas. Despite his logical emphasis on local culture, Renzo Piano

A section drawing showing a
typical structural configuration.

Below
A partially covered walkway
links the pavilions.

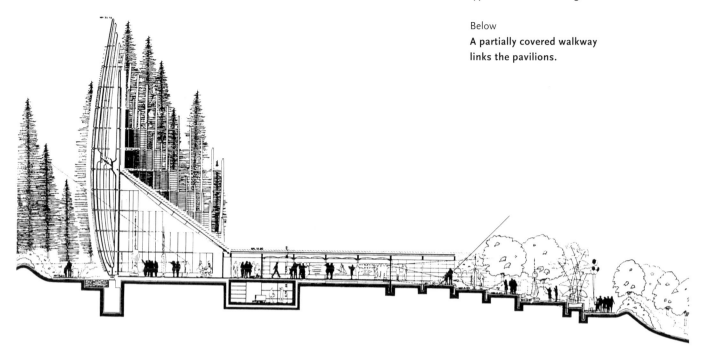

An aerial view of the complex, which sits alone on a green peninsula.

Below
An overall plan of the complex.

here blends the use of wood and natural ventilation with glass and aluminum elements. A visit to the Center is conceived as a stroll through the carefully preserved tropical environment. One quality that sets Renzo Piano apart from other talented architects is his ability to adapt his designs to their locations while maintaining a constant interest in materials and appropriate technology. Even when using metaphors, Piano varies his approach. Where the roof of Kansai Airport can be said to resemble a wing, the pavilions of the Jean-Marie Tjibaou Center are as much like sails as they are reminiscent of local hut design. His subtle references are never so literal as to become obvious. A master of modern, abstract architecture, he nonetheless succeeds in adapting his architecture to the most varied sites and functions.

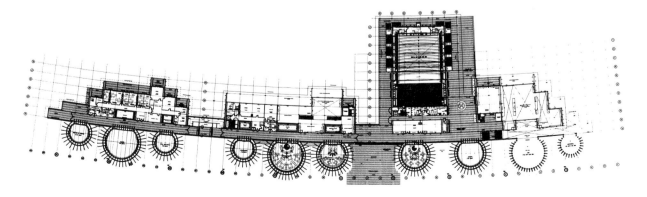

1992–2000 ▸ Potsdamer Platz Reconstruction

Berlin, Germany

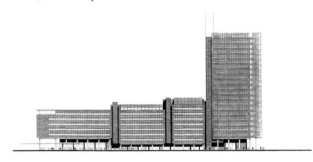

Seen from the exterior, the buildings are typically light and modern—Piano's contribution to Berlin's reconstruction.

Top
An elevation drawing shows the different elements of the complex.

Opposite page
Inside the theater and casino building.

The reconstruction of Berlin's Potsdamer Platz was one of the most ambitious urban development programs of the late 20th century. Destroyed during World War II and the later construction of the Berlin Wall, plans for reconstruction of the square began in 1990 with the organization of a competition for the site south of the Tiergarten, east of Scharoun's Preussischer Staatsbibliothek and west of Leipziger Platz. A master plan by Hilmer & Sattler was chosen and individual landowners began to select architects. Daimler-Benz picked Renzo Piano for their master plan and for the construction projects on five of the 15 planned sites. Piano determined the general configuration of the streets and buildings and stipulated that all of the structures should have copper roofs, and use clear glass and materials resembling terra-cotta for façades. RPBW worked here in association with Christoph Kohlbecker. Other architects involved in these projects included Rafael Moneo, Arata Isozaki, Richard Rogers, and Hans Kollhoff. The first completed project by Piano was the Debis Headquarters, a 45000-square-meter building made to look like four structures rather than one. Although it contains a monumental 28-meter-high atrium, one of the most remarkable features of the Debis Headquarters is the double-skin glass façade design for the east, south, and west elevations of the 21-story-high tower. A layer of pivoting glass panels is set 70 centimeters outside the inner glass wall. Opened by a system of sensors during warm weather, the double skin obviates the need for excessive air conditioning. Terra-cotta screens are used on the outer layer of the lower sections of the complex. An IMAX theater designed by the Renzo Piano Building Workshop faces the rear of the Debis block, reinforcing the urban continuity established by the architect, despite the insistence of one architect to use other materials for the façades of the neighboring Hyatt Hotel. The convertible IMAX theater, also known by the name B7, is a 15600-square-meter mixed-use building including the theater, a restaurant, and retail spaces. The 440-seat theater is located in a sphere 36 meters in diameter that is integrated into the building. The spherical volume of the theater rises above the building and is visible from a distance. The sphere is also visible from the street through a 1000-square-meter clear glass façade.

1991–1997 ▸ Beyeler Foundation

Riehen (Basel), Switzerland

The walkway leading to the main entrance.

Below
An elevation drawing shows the long,
low form of the building.

Opposite page
Transparent spaces allow visitors to view
sculptures by Alberto Giacometti from outside.

Built on a site close to the German border in the Basel suburb of Riehen, the Beyeler Foundation is an exercise in architectural restraint and mastery. The long, narrow site also includes a park area and connects to a former house serving as a shop, café, and museum offices. Located next to a busy road leading toward the Black Forest, the building is designed with a Patagonian porphyry wall closing off the street side. This stone is also used for other museum areas. Within the galleries, white walls and light wood floors give a degree of the serenity requested by the Foundation's founder, the art dealer Ernst Beyeler. This calm seems to be almost the direct antithesis of the busy "high-tech" approach of the Pompidou Center. An emphasis on natural lighting gives optimal viewing conditions for the impressive collection of Impressionist and modern art accumulated by Beyeler, as well as the numerous works shown during temporary exhibitions. It can be noted that the Beyeler Foundation was completed the same year as the much-vaunted Bilbao Guggenheim by Frank Gehry. It would be difficult for two museum structures to be so different. Where it comes to showing fine works of art in an environment that places them in their best light in every sense of the word, there can be no doubt that the Beyeler Foundation is a far better instrument than Gehry's sculptural fantasy. Rather than seeking to express his own artistic ambitions, Renzo Piano has wisely chosen to reflect the wishes of his client and to honor the artworks the Beyeler Foundation contains. Though he may have garnered fewer articles in the press, Renzo Piano's achievement here is more in tune with the times than the explosively heroic approach seen in Bilbao.

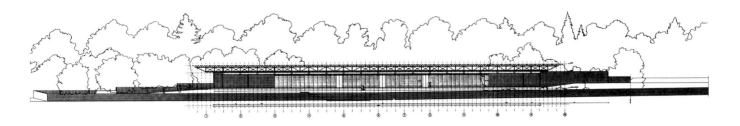

1997–2001 ▸ Niccolò Paganini Auditorium

Parma, Italy

Seen from the exterior, the structure looks like an almost empty shell.

Below right
A sketch by Piano showing the main auditorium at the center.

Opposite page
A night view of the building with its internal structure fully visible.

The Paganini Auditorium was built inside the former Eridania sugar factory, a heterogeneous group of industrial buildings. Set near the historical center of Parma, the area is now a park, known for its tree and shrub specimens. Despite its original function, the main building was well proportioned from an acoustical point of view, and Piano took the unusual liberty of eliminating the transversal walls, replacing them with three large glass façades. A system of soundproof panels hung from the trusses over the stage participates in the spatial organization of the main area. Even though the building is 90 meters long, the use of glazing permits it to be transparent from the outside and allows guests not to lose sight of the park. Leading to the entrance, a row of double lanterns frames the approach path. The public enters through the south end of the building, and proceeds through the building's length. A first high-roofed, open-air space leads inside, passing through a wide glass wall. From this point, visitors continue on to the two-level foyer. Located at the north end, the 250-square-meter stage offers enough space for large musical ensembles, including a choir and orchestra. In a most unusual configuration, the rear of this stage is nothing other than a glass wall, giving an almost unimpeded view of the park beyond. The 780 seats are set on a slightly sloping surface covering an area of 590 square meters, ensuring good visibility from all seats. Other former factory units were used for the service and rehearsal spaces.

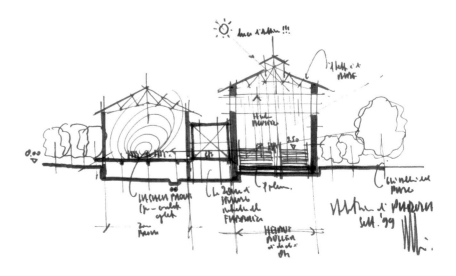

1998–2001 ▸ Maison Hermès

Tokyo, Japan

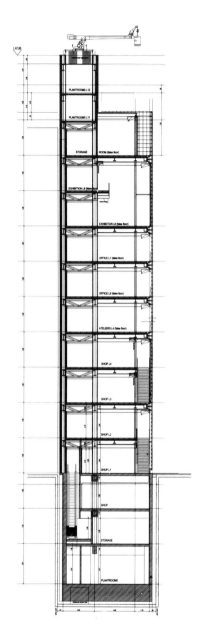

It may be significant that Renzo Piano's projects outside of his native Italy are rarely isolated cases. Well after the completion of the Kansai International Airport terminal, he remains a highly respected figure in Japan, and it is not surprising that the French fashion house Hermès called on him for their flagship store located in the Ginza area of Tokyo. The most striking feature of the 44.55-meter-high structure is its façade made of 13 000 45 x 45-centimeter glass blocks. Made by Vetroarredo in Florence, with supports manufactured in Switzerland and installed in Japan, the glass blocks are a successful example of international collaboration in contemporary architecture. The glass blocks were specially manufactured to meet stringent Japanese fire and earthquake standards. Each block is intended to be able to move as much as four millimeters, absorbing any potential seismic shock. Conceived of as a "magic lantern" particularly because of its luminous nighttime appearance, the structure may recall such modern icons as Pierre Chareau's Maison de Verre, but it also retains a distinctly Japanese flavor. The filtered views of the outside world seen from within are images from a floating, liquid world. There is a lightness in this glass wall that brings to mind the best of Japan's traditional architecture. On a 580-square-meter site, the architect has built a 6071-square-meter building, with some 1150 square meters used for actual sales areas. The building also includes a large space for temporary exhibitions and a small "museum" of the history of the house of Hermès (designed by Hilton McConnico). There are 10 stories above ground, and three below. As fashion houses call more and more on well-known international architects for their boutiques in Tokyo, particularly in the Ginza and Omotesando areas, Renzo Piano's Maison Hermès will stand out as an exceptional blend of European modernity and Japanese perception.

A section drawing exposes the narrow floor design.

Opposite page
The transparent glass-block building stands out in this night view of Ginza.

1994–2002 ▸ Parco della Musica Auditorium

Rome, Italy

An aerial view of the entire complex.

Opposite page
The closed, shell-like lead cladding of the buildings.

Below
A section drawing shows how the roof envelops the concert space.

In his first project in Rome, Renzo Piano set out to create "a city dedicated to music." Located in the Quartiere Olimpico created for the 1960 Summer Olympics, on the main road leading into Rome from the north, the complex proved its adaptability early in the construction process when the ruins of a fourth-century farmhouse villa were discovered on the site. This discovery held up work for a year and had to be integrated as a museum into the final design. Piano rotated the entire design and moved it six meters to the north to accommodate this discovery. The complex is made up of three lead-covered auditoriums respectively seating 2800, 1200, and 750 people, and each facing a 3000-seat outdoor amphitheater. The first of these, the largest of its kind in Europe, is designed for symphonic concerts, and like the smaller ones boasts a good deal of flexibility, for example in stage configurations. The 1200-seat hall is meant for ballets and contemporary music, while the smallest facility will be used for operas, baroque music, and theater. The acoustics of the facility were worked out by Helmut Müller in collaboration with Pierre Boulez and Luciano Berio. Piano has stated that he had Hans Scharoun's Berlin Philharmonic and Library in mind in designing the Roman structures. Opened officially by Walter Veltroni, the mayor of Rome, on April 21, 2002 (though not yet fully completed at that time), the complex is surrounded by three hectares of park area newly planted with 400 trees.

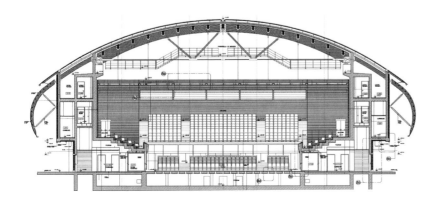

1996–2000 ▸ Aurora Place

Sydney, Australia

the two hats
are the same.

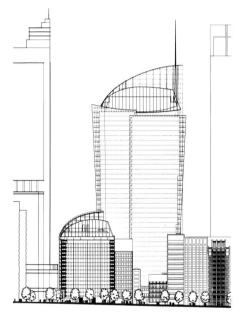

An elevation drawing shows the configuration of Aurora Place vis-à-vis neighboring buildings.

Right
A transparent glass façade opens toward the Royal Botanic Garden.

Opposite page
Piano's building stands out in this view from the Garden.

Aurora Place is a mixed-use project situated near Sydney's Royal Botanic Garden. Two towers, an 18-story residential building, and a 41-story office structure, make up the complex. A light glazed canopy links the two blocks and announces the openness of the design at ground level. A degree of warmth is achieved by the use of glazed terracotta tile cladding where glass panels are not used. Both towers have subtly curved and folded façades that might echo the sail-like forms of Jørn Utzon's nearby Sydney Opera House. Piano's personal interest in sailboats comes to mind here too. Typically, Piano has innovated in the outer shell, using glass panels whose opacity can be varied by changing the size and position of the frit. A good deal of attention is paid to the comfort of users, for example with the winter gardens on the office floors that have operable glass louvers to allow air to come in. In the apartment building, each apartment cuts through the entire floor, giving bedrooms a view toward a plaza, and living rooms overlooking the Royal Botanic Garden. Although the office tower is imposing, with its 49000 square meters of floor space and 200-meter height, the complex remains approachable and "human" in good part because of Piano's close attention to detail and to aspects such as ventilation and sun shading. Set against the background of Sydney's numerous high-rise buildings, Aurora Place fulfills Piano's stated ambition in this case, to make a tower that is "not just a pile of unrelated office slabs, but a real vertical piece of the city."

1999–2003 ▸ Nasher Sculpture Center

Dallas, Texas, USA

As is often the case in the United States, the Nasher Sculpture Center was created at the behest of a wealthy individual, Raymond Nasher. The entire $60 million cost was borne by his foundation. Though a Bostonian, Nasher has long lived in Dallas and made his fortune with shopping centers. An avid collector of modern sculptures, he decided to buy a plot of land adjacent to the Dallas Museum of Art to exhibit his works. Originally a parking lot, the 150 x 60-meter site includes a 4000-square-meter gallery for the more fragile works. The building consists of six travertine marble walls, defining five bays. The three center spaces, covered by a curved glass roof, contain the exhibition spaces, while the other bays and the basement house a bookshop, cafeteria, auditorium, offices, gift shop, and the Nasher Institute for Modern Sculpture. The outdoor exhibition areas are four to five meters below grade, so that the works look as though they had come from an archeological dig. Since it opened in October 2003, it has attracted at least 200 000 visitors. Raymond Nasher was inspired to choose Renzo Piano as his architect in large part because of his admiration for Piano's Menil Collection building, but the two men met at the opening of the Beyeler Foundation in Basel. Nasher, a client of Ernst Beyeler, bought works by Rodin, Miró, Tinguely, Matisse, and Giacometti from the Swiss dealer.

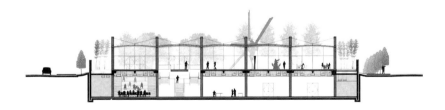

1999–2005 ▸ Zentrum Paul Klee

Bern, Switzerland

A sketch by Renzo Piano reveals the rolling, hill-like form of the design in section.

Below right
The entrance path leading to the Zentrum Paul Klee.

Opposite page
With its arcing form, the architecture assumes a landscape-inspired presence.

The site of the Zentrum Paul Klee is outside Bern, close to the artist's tomb, in a landscape of gently rolling hills, with the Alps in the distance. It was this topography that inspired the design of the museum itself, although the site has been considerably altered due to nearby roads, including a highway leading out of Bern. Intended to house 40 percent of the 10 000 known works of the Swiss artist, the structure is integrated into three artificial hills. The first of these hills contains a 300-seat auditorium and a museum for children. The middle hill contains the main exhibition space, with space for temporary shows below ground. The final volume contains works not on public display and a center for the study of Klee's oeuvre. Due to the sensitivity to light of many of the artist's works, overhead natural light is not really part of this scheme, and part of the roof is covered with vegetation, emphasizing the symbiosis of the architecture with the landscape. That said, Piano pierced the roof at various points to bring in daylight, where the conservation of the works permits. The arches forming the volumes of the complex are clearly inspired by naval construction. As Piano says, the shape of a boat is not dictated by any real concerns of geometry, but rather by the rules of movement through water.

1999–2005 ▸ High Museum of Art Expansion

Atlanta, Georgia, USA

The ribbed design of the exterior of the buildings is echoed in this gallery view.

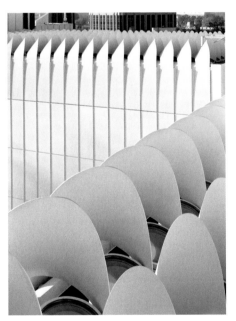

The building's ribs allow light to penetrate while giving an impression of solid forms.

Opposite page
Piano's signature lightness is visible in this plaza view of the expansion.

It was subsequent to the 1962 crash of a plane carrying Atlanta's arts community leaders that Robert Woodruff of the Coca-Cola Company created the Woodruff Foundation. Today, the Woodruff Arts Center includes the Alliance Theatre Company, the High Museum of Art, the Atlanta College of Art, the 14th Street Playhouse, and the Atlanta Symphony Orchestra. The original High Museum was designed by Richard Meier, and opened to the public in 1983. With its central atrium inspired by Frank Lloyd Wright's Guggenheim, the museum includes about 5000 square meters of exhibition space for works which can be viewed from many different angles through the space of the building, and a 200-seat auditorium. Since its completion, the High has nearly doubled the size of its collection and has 500 000 visitors per year. These facts led the Woodruff Arts Center to ask Renzo Piano to add 16 000 square meters of extra facilities, including additional gallery space, enlarged special exhibition areas, and improved visitor amenities. Piano designed three new buildings: a main pavilion, a special collections building, and an administrative office structure. A glass bridge links the main pavilion, with its "expansive, light-filled lobby," to the Meier building at the ground level and the top floor. Piano's plans include other elements of the Woodruff Arts Center campus to create a "pedestrian-friendly village for the arts." As Piano has stated: "In planning the design of the High and the Woodruff Arts Center, we had the challenge of serving the needs of this established museum of fine art, while integrating its design with that of the entire Woodruff Arts Center campus. We set out to create a vision for the entire campus—a dynamic center for art and culture—that would invigorate the people and the cultural life of the city." The total construction budget stood at $163.4 million. Additionally, a $15 million endowment goal had been set, bringing the budget for the entire project to $178.4 million.

2000–2006 ▸ Morgan Library Renovation and Expansion

New York, New York, USA

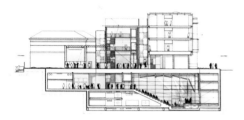

A section drawing showing the auditorium below grade.

Opposite page
Top, the main entrance on Madison Avenue.
Bottom, the interior piazza.

Below right
The new auditorium also seen in section above.

Serving as both a museum and a library, the Morgan Library is home to one of the world's largest and finest collections of rare Medieval and Renaissance literary and musical manuscripts, books, prints, and drawings. Created by the financier J. P. Morgan (1837–1913), the Library was housed in a building designed by New York architects McKim, Mead & White in 1903. The Morgan Library later extended to the Morgan Library Annex Building, built in 1928, and subsequently to a series of other extensions, including the former mansion of the Morgan family (1853). With the goals of rendering this situation more rational and of increasing visitor and storage space, the Library called on RPBW. The architects expanded the Morgan by a third without exceeding the height of the historic structures through digging into the bedrock beneath the Library. A 299-seat auditorium, a three-level storage vault, and mechanical spaces were thus housed below grade in new space. Above ground a new glazed "piazza" creates a sense of unity and coherence between the old and new areas. A new public entrance on Madison Avenue was created, and the existing buildings significantly renovated. A 6-meter cube was added at ground level for displaying masterpieces and as an element uniting the earlier McKim and Annex buildings. A new four-story building directly connected to the Morgan Mansion was added on the north side for offices that face the piazza and 37th Street. The Annex Building was made into the main gallery space, and a new bookshop, café, and small restaurant were also added.

2000–2007 ▸ The New York Times Building

New York, New York, USA

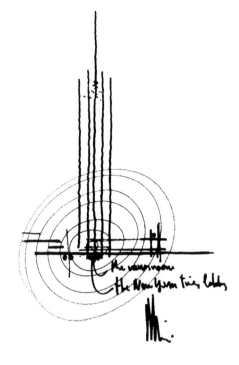

A sketch by Piano with concentric circles around the newsroom.

Below right
The building carries the famous logo of the daily newspaper.

Opposite page
The structure stands out from its setting near Times Square.

According to Renzo Piano: "The New York Times Building, at 8th Avenue and Times Square, has a very strong urban presence. The building is designed to be part of the street on which it stands. On the ground floor, there is a garden and an auditorium. In a way this approach may be more European than American." Chosen over Norman Foster, Frank Gehry, and Cesar Pelli, Piano's design for the 52-story building is intended to be as open and transparent as possible, symbolizing the relationship of the newspaper to the city. The façades employ a combination of clear glass curtain walls and a scrim of white ceramic tubes hanging 61 centimeters outside the glass. Acting as a sunscreen, the tubes obviate the need for tinted or fritted glass. Underway in 2000, and reconfirmed after the attacks on the World Trade Center, the New York Times Building is seen as a sign of confidence and commitment to the city. The newspaper occupies the lower half of the structure while a real-estate development firm, Forest City Ratner, is commercializing the rest of the space. The six-story base of the tower includes an atrium for shops and restaurants and an auditorium for lectures. A roof garden is protected by extensions of the glass curtain wall above the actual building height. *The New York Times* has had several locations in Manhattan, including its tower on 42nd Street opened on January 1, 1905, and its most recent structure, on West 43rd Street, modified three times since its 1913 completion. Because of its considerable height, central location, and vocation, the New York Times Building is one of the most prestigious commissions to be given to a foreign architect in recent years in Manhattan.

2000–2008 ▸ California Academy of Sciences Renovation and Expansion

San Francisco, California, USA

The green roof of the building is one of its most remarkable features.

Right
Seen from a distance, the Academy seems to blend into its green setting.

Opposite page
A light canopy shelters a walkway in a typical gesture by Renzo Piano.

This large project was completed in late 2007, but the work of installing the museum went on into 2008. The project had a total budget, including exhibition facilities, of $370 million. Founded in 1853, the California Academy of Sciences is housed in 12 buildings, built without a master plan over a period of 80 years, beginning in 1916. It is the only combined Aquarium, Planetarium, and Natural History Museum in the United States and is located in Golden Gate Park. It was in 1989, when some of the facilities were damaged in the Loma Prieta earthquake, that the Academy began its plans to upgrade the facilities. Piano's plan includes a "village-like cluster of spaces under a contoured roof." The environmentally friendly roof, measuring about 1.5 hectares, is covered with vegetation, making the new building "almost a piece of the park," according to the architect. A partially glass-enclosed piazza forms the central space of the completed project. Renzo Piano worked with the local architects Gordon Chong & Partners on this project, in which only one of the existing buildings, the neoclassical beaux-arts Africa Hall, was restored. Other historic features of the Academy, such as the barrel-vaulted ceiling of the Steinhart Aquarium and the North American hall, are, however, evoked in the new complex. The whole "incorporates environmentally responsible construction technology and recycled and renewable building materials into an aesthetically accomplished master plan." Large windows offer views toward the park, but Piano's design actually reduced the "footprint" of the complex by making more

Vegetation is also present within the domed spaces lit by circular skylights.

Below
Like the "Bolla" on the Lingotto Factory, a spherical form animates the interior volume.

The entrance to the expansion where a bridge provides access to the warm interior.

Below
A section drawing showing the relation of the green roof to the internal spaces.

efficient use of interior space and employing underground construction. As opposed to completely distinct areas, the Academy "features flexible, integrated exhibition spaces that reflect the interconnections of the living world and the multidisciplinary nature of science."

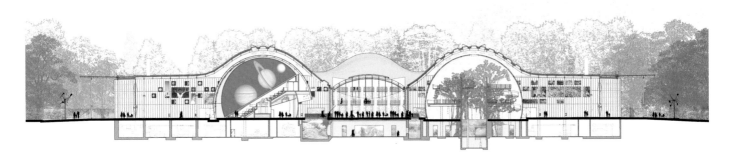

2000–2009 ▸ Modern Wing of the Art Institute of Chicago

Chicago, Illinois, USA

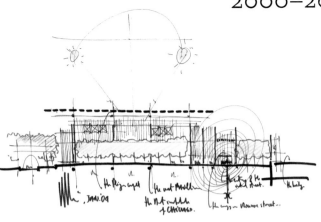

A sketch by Piano showing the simple form with the projecting roof of the new Wing.

Below
Transparency is skillfully combined with the protective nature required of art exhibition buildings.

Opposite page
Both light and airy, the modernity of Piano is fully visible in this image.

The city of Chicago has embarked on a large-scale cultural program centered on the lakefront Millennium Park, a 10-hectare former zone of railway tracks and parking lots. Frank Gehry has designed a 200-meter-long trellis and a band shell for the park, while Renzo Piano has been called on to build a $200 million addition to the Art Institute of Chicago. His L-shaped building is replacing the former Goodman Theatre at the corner of Columbus and Monroe. Using glass, steel, and limestone, Piano has carefully thought out the connection between the old and the new—the old being the original 19th-century beaux-arts museum buildings. A "minimalist" pedestrian bridge across Monroe Street will connect the park to the cultural facility. The 25000-square-meter addition will have what has been called a "flying carpet" roof. Though this design is seen locally as being a complement to Gehry's pavilion in the park, this airy form of roof is also seen in the Pinacoteca recently added to the Lingotto factory in Turin. With the development of Millennium Park, the Art Institute of Chicago, one of America's richest museums, will be located between two green areas, since it is also close to Grant Park. An essential element of the program was that the new structure links the two older existing buildings, straddling a railway line. Piano refers to immense railroad tracks as being the starting point of his inspiration for this structure. In an interesting homage to a great Chicago architect, Renzo Piano has proposed to relocate the entrance arch of Louis Sullivan's demolished Chicago Stock Exchange Building (formerly at the southwest corner of Monroe and Columbus) closer to the museum's preserved and renovated Stock Exchange Trading Room.

This gallery view shows the Chicago
skyline with Frank Gehry's band shell
in the exterior foreground.

A section drawing shows the relation
of the interior of the Wing with the bridge
that extends into the park.

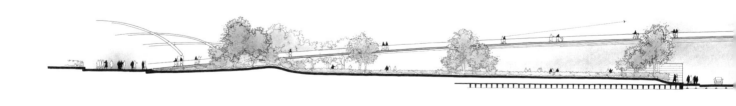

The new building seen from beneath the
bridge that leads to Millennium Park.

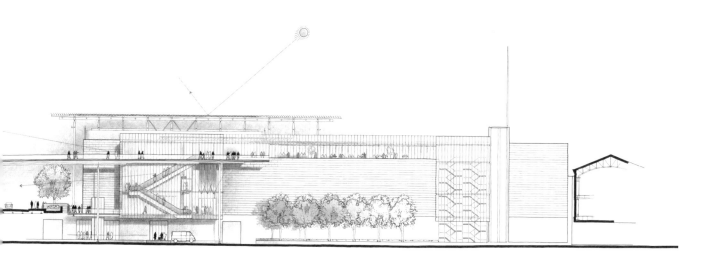

2002–2010 ▸ Central Saint Giles Mixed-Use Development

London, UK

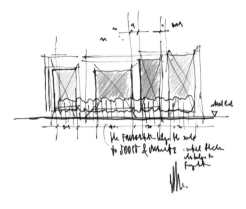

A sketch by Renzo Piano shows the brightly colored blocks that make up the complex.

Below

An aerial view with the residential building to the bottom of the image (left) and a drawing showing the final version of the scheme (right).

The Central Saint Giles Mixed-Use Development in London includes 56 apartments, 53 "affordable" flats, 37 000 square meters of office space, and a public piazza with a restaurant and retail spaces, on a 7000-square-meter site. The residential tower was acquired and completed by United House Developments. The buildings are marked by their colorful façades, made up of 134 000 green, orange, lime, and yellow glazed terracotta tiles. Renzo Piano states: "The color idea came from observing the sudden surprise given by brilliant colors in that part of the city. Cities should not be boring or repetitive. One of the reasons cities are so beautiful and a great idea is that they are full of surprises, the idea of color represents a joyful surprise." The buildings are grounded around a courtyard in the center of the site, open to the exterior by pedestrian paths. The project received an award for the Best Commercial Workspace from the British Council for Offices (BCO, 2011). The complex was completed in May 2010, and is located near the east end of Oxford Street where an office building erected in the 1950s was formerly occupied by the Ministry of Defence. The new complex includes a 15-story west block with the 109 residential units, and the larger 11-story eastern block for offices featuring the largest floor plates of any office building in West London. Though originally somewhat controversial, the colorful complex has attracted such prestigious office clients as NBCUniversal and Google.

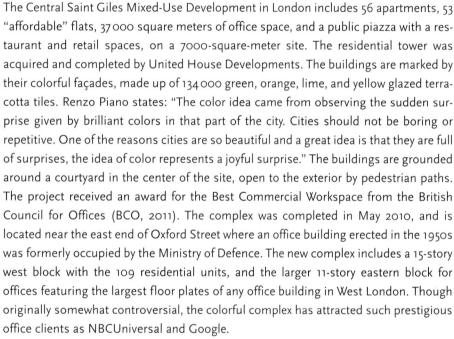
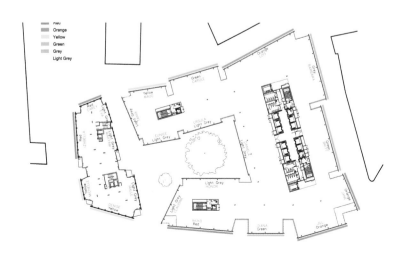

2003–2010 ▸ Los Angeles County Museum of Art (BCAM and the Resnick Pavilion)

Los Angeles, California, USA

The exterior escalator of the BCAM.

Below
An elevation drawing of the Broad Contemporary Art Museum (BCAM).

Opposite page
The travertine-clad façade of the BCAM with its signature red elements, and the suspended external stairway supported by cables.

The Los Angeles County Museum of Art (LACMA) is situated on an eight-hectare plot of land including 10 buildings. Renzo Piano was the project architect for the program (with Gensler acting as Executive Architect) called "Transformation" which included the Broad Contemporary Art Museum (BCAM, 2008) and the Lynda and Stewart Resnick Exhibition Pavilion, completed in 2010. The BCAM has 5574 square meters of gallery space, and the BP Grand Entrance, which is a 750-square-meter open-air pavilion and orientation space. The roof of this pavilion includes solar panels intended to power a work by Chris Burden called *Urban Light*. Located north of the BCAM, the Resnick Pavilion is a 4180-square-meter structure. Clad in Italian travertine, the BCAM features a red "spider" escalator on its north façade. The Resnick Pavilion, built at a cost of $53 million on top of a parking garage, has an open floor plan with concrete floors and a sawtooth roof with vertical glazing. LACMA bills the Pavilion as "the largest purpose-built, naturally lit open-plan museum space in the world." The eastern and western walls of the Resnick Pavilion are clad in pale travertine marble that comes from the same quarry as the marble used for the BCAM's façade. To the north and south, Renzo Piano has used glass cladding. The mechanical systems and exterior technical rooms of the Pavilion are colored in the same "Renzo Red" used for the BCAM escalator. Piano said of the overall LACMA master plan: "If you are designing a museum you offer contemplation. It is not enough for the light to be perfect. You also need calm, serenity, and even a voluptuous quality linked to contemplation of the work of art. Achieving such a result at the Los Angeles County Museum of Art depends on integrating the new museum into its broader context. That is the purpose of a master plan."

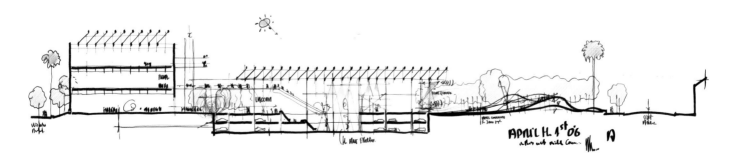

2000–2012 ▸ The Shard – London Bridge Tower

London, UK

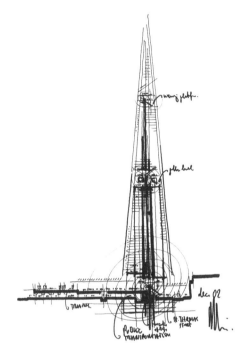

A sketch by Renzo Piano showing the main elements of the tower.

Below
The London skyline with St Paul's on the left and Tate Modern on the right.

Opposite page
A photo of the nearly completed tower in its urban setting.

In March 2002, Southwark Borough Council gave permission to build a £350 million, 66-story tower above the London Bridge tube station. The 305-meter-tall structure will be Europe's tallest office building. With nearly 90 000 square meters of space, it will contain offices, hotels, restaurants, and apartments. Dubbed the "Spike" or "Shard of Glass," the building has elicited considerable controversy but won over the support of London's then mayor, Ken Livingstone. Though economic conditions and events such as the September 11 attack in New York may give some second thoughts about the construction of such visible towers, Renzo Piano strongly defends the idea. His own statement, made in November 2000, makes it clear why. "This is my vision," he says, "I see the tower like a vertical little town for about 10 000 people to work in and enjoy and for hundreds of thousands more to commute to and from. This is why we have included shops, museums, offices, restaurants, and residential spaces within its 66 floors. The shape of the tower is generous at the bottom without arrogantly touching the ground, and narrow at the top, disappearing in the air like a 16th-century pinnacle or the mast top of a very tall ship.... Symbols," he continues, "are dangerous. Often tall buildings are aggressive and arrogant symbols of power and ego, selfish and hermetic. I don't even think we should strive to be the tallest building in Europe but this may happen naturally. One thing is certain: the tower is designed to be a sharp and light presence in the London skyline. Architecture is about telling stories and expressing visions, and memory is part of it. Our memory is permeated by history. That is why this design alludes to spires. One final important point," concludes Renzo Piano, "St Paul's Cathedral is an extraordinary monument and an intrinsic part of London's heritage. I believe that the new tower will not disturb its stateliness. They are breathing the same air, sharing the same atmosphere; they are nurtured at the same source."

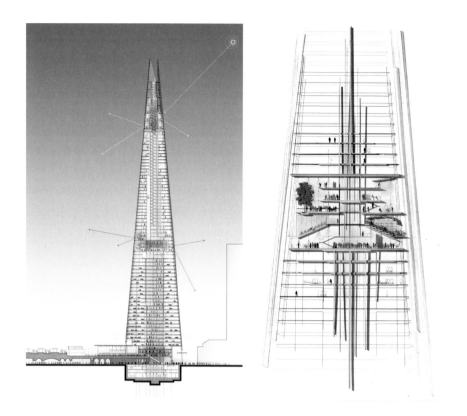

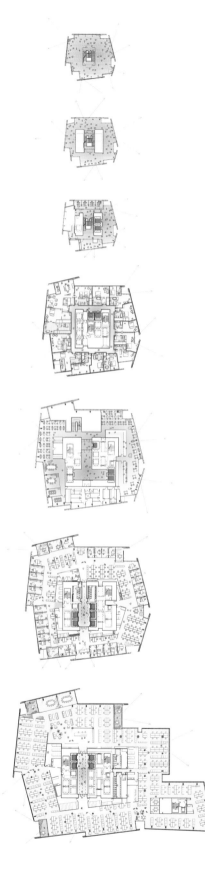

Opposite
Elevation drawings and plans show
the tapering form of the tower, with the
uppermost levels considerably smaller
than the bottom ones. A photo shows the
building rising above London.

Right
The glass walls rise up above the highest
level of the building, giving the impression
of a fragmented continuity.

Below
At its base, the tower appears to be
lifted up off the ground, making way for
the heavily used London Bridge station.

2006–2012 ▸ Astrup Fearnley Museum of Modern Art

Oslo, Norway

Partially covered walkways add to the convivial aspect of the complex.

Opposite page
The presence of a canal recalls the proximity of the harbor and links to a nearby development area.

Right
A section drawing shows how the curving roof links the two elements seen here with the canal running between the buildings.

This project was carried out by RPBW in collaboration with Narud Stokke Wiig. It was designed between 2006 and 2009 and built between 2009 and the summer of 2012. The total floor area of the project is 15 600 square meters, including offices and an art museum. Located southwest of the center of Oslo, it is a continuation of the Aker Brygge development completed in the 1990s. The site of the Tjuvholmen project is considered one of the most beautiful places in Oslo. The project aims to "transform the formerly closed harbor into a public area connecting the fjord and the center of the city." It includes three buildings located under a single curved 6000-square-meter glass roof: one for offices and the exhibition of art, and the other two for an art museum. The architects explain: "The design strongly identifies the project. Its curved shape, formed by laminated wood beams, crosses the canal between the buildings. The beams are supported by slender steel columns, reinforced with cable rigging, which refer to the maritime character of the site. The roof's geometrical shape is derived from a toroid (a doughnut-shaped object) and it slopes down toward the sea." The continuity of the quay of the canal leading to the tip of the new development is very much part of the design thinking, allowing "a spectacular view out over the fjord, but also back to the center of Oslo." An 800-meter canal promenade links Aker Brygge to the new complex. A sculpture park is located between the museum and the sea with works by Louise Bourgeois, Ellsworth Kelly, Anish Kapoor, Franz West, Paul McCarthy, and Antony Gormley among others. The exhibition spaces of the art museum on the north side of the canal house a permanent contemporary art collection. The building on the south side of the canal is for temporary exhibitions. The four-story office building has a naturally lit atrium in the center. Weathered timber is used on the opaque façade areas of the complex, with reference to Scandinavian traditions.

2010–2012 ▸ Auditorium del Parco

L'Aquila, Italy

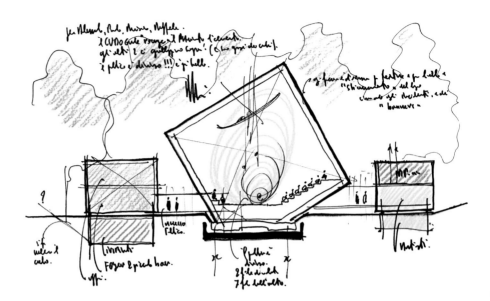

Right
A section sketch by Renzo Piano, with his usual manuscript remarks, outlines the basic form of the complex.

Right
A section sketch by Renzo Piano, with his usual manuscript remarks, outlines the basic form of the complex.

Above
A night view emphasizes the playful color scheme of the auditorium, and the notched and interpenetrating nature of the main cubic volumes.

Opposite page
The colorful pattern of the larch-clad exterior brings to mind a musical composition and also a bit of gaiety in a town that was severely tested by the 2009 earthquake.

The earthquake that struck L'Aquila in the Abruzzo region of Italy on April 6, 2009, destroyed the city's auditorium, since then it has been undergoing a slow reconstruction process. With the financial support of the Autonomous Province of Trento, RPBW proposed a temporary solution: three striped wooden cubes were built, forming a public plaza on the grounds of a medieval castle in just eight months with the help of local students. The facility opened in October 2012. The architects explain that "larch from Trento was famously used by Stradivarius and other 17th-century master luthiers, and here larch panels have been used to create an auditorium that will resonate like a giant musical instrument. Timber construction is also known to be significantly earthquake resistant, which makes the concert hall a useful prototype for cost-effective reconstruction in L'Aquila's city center." The cube exteriors are clad in 25-centimeter-wide, four-centimeter-thick larch tiles. The largest cube sits at a 45-degree angle to provide raked seating for 240 people. Raw wood surfaces hung with acoustic panels assure that up to 40 musicians can be well heard in the space. To the right of the auditorium, another cube contains a box office, café, and toilets. To the left, the third cube offers space for the performers, including dressing rooms. Glazed corridors connect the three cubes. Piano emphasizes the importance of the central plaza as a meeting place for residents of the devastated city. The outdoor area facing the auditorium's volume can be fitted with seating, making it possible for about 500 people to attend open-air performances or follow concert activities on large temporary screens in the summer.

2007–2013 ► Kimbell Art Museum Expansion

Fort Worth, Texas, USA

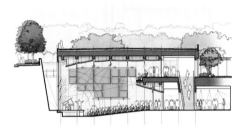

Recognized as one of the masterpieces of modern architecture, Louis Kahn's 1972 Kimbell Art Museum near downtown Fort Worth posed a particular challenge to Renzo Piano and his team. The so-called Piano Pavilion has a floor area of 7595 square meters as opposed to the 11 148-square-meter size of the original Kahn building. The new structure adds 1505 square meters of gallery space, an education center, auditorium, and library, as well as parking space. Alabaster-toned architectural concrete, laminated Douglas fir ceiling beams, and quarter-sawn engineered white oak flooring are the main visible materials, together with double-glazed, gas-filled glass. The architects explain: "Echoing Kahn's building in height, scale, and general layout, the RPBW building has a more open, transparent character. Light, discreet (half the footprint is hidden underground), yet with its own character, setting up a dialogue between old and new, the new building consists of two connected structures. The front section, facing the west façade of Kahn's building across landscaped grounds, has a three-part façade, referencing the activities inside. At its center, a lightweight, transparent glazed section serves as the new museum entrance. On either side, behind pale concrete walls, are two gallery spaces for temporary exhibitions. A colonnade of square concrete columns wraps around the sides of the building, supporting solid wooden beams and the overhanging eaves of the glass roof, providing shade for the glazed façades facing north and south." A green roof, photovoltaic cells, geothermal wells, and low-energy LED lighting contribute to the overall energy efficiency of the new building. The Kimbell Art Museum is located across the street from Tadao Ando's Modern Art Museum of Fort Worth (2002).

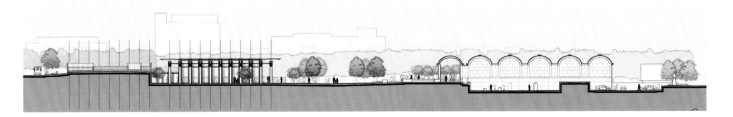

2007–2015 ‣ The Whitney Museum of American Art

New York, New York, USA

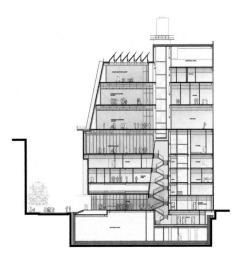

After numerous efforts to renovate and enlarge their Madison Avenue building (Marcel Breuer, 1966) the Whitney Museum of American Art decided to relocate to a new downtown building designed by RPBW. The nine-story building has a projected cost of $422 million, and will offer a total of 4645 square meters of interior exhibition space, to which a further 1207 square meters will be added on the exterior. The new structure, including education facilities and a 170-seat theater, as well as the usual public areas, is located at Washington and Gansevoort Streets in Manhattan. The cantilevered main entrance is near the southern entrance of the High Line Park and adds 790 square meters to the public spaces at this location. The structural steel was topped out in December 2012, and the museum opened in May 2015. The Whitney states that the asymmetrical form of the structure corresponds to "the industrial character of neighboring buildings and the neighboring High Line." Built with concrete, steel, stone, reclaimed pine, and low-iron glass, the structure seeks to be New York City's first certified LEED Gold art museum. The new building is, in fact, in some sense returning closer to its roots, since it was founded in Greenwich Village in 1930 by Gertrude Vanderbilt Whitney. With his other New York work, including the New York Times Building and the expansion and renovation of the Morgan Library, Piano has taken a significant place in the cultural development of the city.

The new Whitney Museum of American
Art seen from the Hudson River side,
where it is somewhat more closed than
on the opposite façade.

Below
An elevation drawing shows the river
on the left and the generous public
entrance area at ground level.

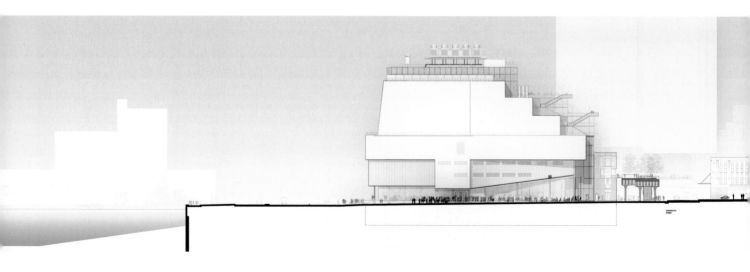

Above
Exhibition galleries continue the relatively "industrial" impression given intentionally by the architect, as expressed here in the way the ceiling is finished.

Right
Outdoor terraces at the upper levels allow visitors to view sculptures, but also to look down on the Meatpacking District and nearby High Line Park.

Life and Work

Renzo Piano was born in September 1937 in Genoa, Italy. He studied in Florence and in Milan, where he worked in the office of Franco Albini and experienced the first student rebellions of the 1960s. Born into a family of builders, frequent visits to his father Carlo's building sites gave him the opportunity to combine practical and academic experience. He graduated from the Politecnico University in Milan in 1964.

From 1965 to 1970, he combined his first experimental work with his brother Ermanno together with numerous trips to the UK and the US.

In 1971, he set up the Piano & Rogers office in London with Richard Rogers. Together they won the competition for the Pompidou Center and he subsequently moved to Paris. From the early 1970s to the 1990s, he worked with the engineer Peter Rice, sharing the Atelier Piano & Rice from 1977 to 1981.

In 1981, the Renzo Piano Building Workshop (RPBW) was established, and it currently has a staff of 150 and offices in Paris, Genoa, and New York. RPBW has designed buildings all around the world. Current projects include the redevelopment and enlargement of the Harvard Art Museums in Cambridge, the Campus of Columbia University in New York, and the Stavros Niarchos Foundation Cultural Center in Athens.

Since 2004 he has also been working for the Renzo Piano Foundation, a non-profit organization dedicated to the promotion of the architectural profession through educational programs and educational activities. The new headquarters was established in Punta Nave (Genoa), in June 2008. In September 2013 Renzo Piano was appointed senator for life by the Italian President Giorgio Napolitano and in May 2014 he received the Columbia University Honorary Degree.

Married to Milly, he lives in Paris and has four children: Carlo, Matteo, Lia, and Giorgio.

Staff

Partners: Renzo Piano, Bernard Plattner, Mark Carroll, Antoine Chaaya, Philippe Goubet, Joost Moolhuijzen, Antonio Belvedere, Elisabetta Trezzani, Giorgio Bianchi, Giorgio Grandi, Emanuela Baglietto. **Associates:** Jack Carter, Paolo Colonna, Christophe Colson, Ivan Corte, Olaf de Nooyer, Kendall Doerr, Emanuele Donadel, Serge Drouin, Catherine Fleury, Alain Gallissian, Stefano Giorgio-Marrano, Vassily Laffineur, Domenico Magnano, Nayla Mecattaf, Jean-Bernard Mothes, Daniele Piano, Antonio Porcile, Dominique Rat, Thorsten Sahlmann, Kevin Schorn, Anne-Hélène Temenides, Erik Volz. **Consultants:** Shunji Ishida, Flavio Marano, Maria Salerno, Alain Vincent. **Architects:** Collin Anderson, Claudio Antonini, William Antozzi, Juan-Pablo Azares, Simon Bastien, Carla Baumann, Francesca Becchi, David Bricard, Hubert Brouta, Paolo Carignano, Paola Carrera, Silvia Casarotto, Velmourougane Chandrasegar, Gounaud Chung, Stefano Cimino, Sebastien Cloarec, Kattalin Del Valle, Sebastian Doerflinger, Ronan Dunphy, Paolo Fang, Daniele Franceschin, Maximilien Forget, Elies Garnaoui, Francesco Giacobello, Albert Giralt, Sara Goiria, Blanche Granet, Nicolas Grawitz, Amaury Greig, Bernardo Grilli, Charles Guézet, John Hallock, Daniel Hammerman, Hugo Houplain, Jonathan Jones, Eleni Kalamakidou, Dafni Karaiskaki, Abigail Karcher, Simone Lafranconi , Maxime Laurent, Audrey McKee, Darius Maïkoff, Michael Matthews, Carolyn Maxwell-Mahon, Alessandra Merli, Serena Minacci, Marco Monti, Emily Murphy, Hiroko Nakatani, Patrycja Ogonowska, Elena Ona, Mara Ottonello, Thomas Niederkorn, Matidia Pallini, Raffaella Parodi, Jean Pattinson, Jeffrey Pauling, Paolo Pelanda, Lorenzo Piazza, Marie Pimmel, Sara Polotti, Luigi Priano, Alisa Rinderspacher, Paul Rizzoti, Gerardo Rosenzweig, Milly Rossato-Piano, Andres Rubio, Stefano Russo, Valerio Sibona, Luciano Simonelli, Manuel Sismondini, Toby Stewart, Boriana Tchonkova, Emmanuel Thireau, Teddy Touma, Robert Tse, Arthur Van Peteghem, Roberto Vinante, Tyler Wilcox, Zoey Wu, Alessandro Zanguio, Jiali Zhou. **IT:** Hocine Bendjama, Pierre Roscelli. **BIM Management:** Daniel Hurtubise, Giuseppe Semprini. **Model-makers & 3D-images:** Olivier Aubert, Fausto Cappellini, Dimitri Lange, Yiorgos Kyrkos, Francesco Terranova, Alessandro Pizzolato. **Documentation & Archives:** Stefania Canta, Chiara Casazza, Giovanna Langasco, Elena Spadavecchia. **Finance & Administration:** Cristina Calvi, Linda Zunino, Evelyne Quach, Antonin Teil. **Secretarial Department:** Francesca Bianchi, Daniela Cappuzzo, Julien Gourrand, Anne-Cécile Guthmann, Francesca Manfredi, Vivian Morosi, Sylvie Romet-Milanesi.

Renzo Piano with his staff from the Genoa, Paris, and New York offices, gathering at the Shard, London, in September 2012.

Photograph by Michel Denancé

Partners

Bernard Plattner (Partner, Director), born in Bern in 1946, studied at the ETH, and started working with Piano & Rogers on the Pompidou Center; continues to work with Renzo Piano in Paris. A Partner since 1989, his projects include the Rue de Meaux Housing, Beyeler Foundation Museum, Potsdamer Platz, Zentrum Paul Klee, New York Times Building, and Pathé Foundation. He is now responsible for the new Courthouse in Paris, a mixed-use development in Vienna, and the Float office building in Düsseldorf.

Mark Carroll (Partner, Director) was born in Hartford, USA, in 1956. He received both his BS and his MS in Architecture from Clemson University. He joined the Genoa office in 1981 working on the Menil Collection. A Partner since 1992, he worked on the Cy Twombly Pavilion, Aurora Place, High Museum expansion, California Academy of Sciences, Harvard Art Museums, expansion of the Kimbell Art Museum, and Whitney Museum of American Art. He is currently working on headquarters for JNBY in Hangzhou, China; the Centro Botín in Santander; and Academy of Motion Picture Arts and Sciences Museum in Los Angeles.

Antoine Chaaya (Partner, Director), born in Lebanon in 1960, studied architecture at the Holy Spirit University of Kaslik (Lebanon), and joined the Paris office in 1987. He worked as lead architect on the Kanak Cultural Center and Potsdamer Platz. A Partner since 1997, he has been responsible for the "Il Sole 24 Ore" headquarters and Los Angeles County Museum of Art expansion. Current projects include academic buildings for Columbia University, a residential project in Miami, and a mixed-use development in Beirut.

Philippe Goubet (Partner, Director) was born in France in 1964 and studied business administra-

tion at the HEC in Paris. He joined RPBW in 1989, working in Genoa as a controller. From 1988 to 1992, he also spent time in Japan, supervising the Osaka office's day-to-day business. In 1995, he moved to RPBW's Paris office and became a Partner. He is currently the Managing Director of the three offices.

Joost Moolhuijzen (Partner, Director), born in Amstelveen, Netherlands, in 1960, studied at Delft University of Technology, and then joined RPBW's Paris office in 1990, working on the Cité Internationale and Potsdamer Platz. A Partner since 1997, he has overseen the Modern Wing of the Art Institute of Chicago and master plan for Columbia University's Manhattanville development, and was partner-in-charge of the Shard. He is now responsible for the Fubon Tower in Taipei and a mixed-use residential project in London.

Antonio Belvedere (Partner, Director), born in 1969, graduated in architecture from the University of Florence. He joined RPBW's Paris office in 1999, working on the Fiat Lingotto Factory, and then as lead architect on the master plan for Columbia University's Manhattanville development. Becoming an Associate in 2004, he worked on the master plan for the ex-Falck area in Milan. He became a Partner in 2011. Recently completed projects include Valletta City Gate. He is now leading the design of the Bishop Ranch in California, a performing arts center in India, and a cultural project in Russia.

Elisabetta Trezzani (Partner, Director), born in 1968, studied at the Politecnico (Milan), graduating in 1994. She joined RPBW in Genoa in 1998, working on the design of Aurora Place and the High Museum. A Partner since

2011, together with M. Carroll, she led the teams working on the Whitney Museum of American Art and Harvard Art Museums. She is currently working on the SoHo residential tower and Academy of Motion Picture Arts and Sciences Museum.

Giorgio Grandi (Partner), born in 1957, studied at the Genoa School of Architecture, and joined RPBW (Genoa) in 1984. He was lead architect on the re-development of Genoa Harbor. A Partner since 1992, he was responsible for the Padre Pio Pilgrimage Church, Banca Popolare di Lodi, and Pirelli Factory. Current projects include the master plan for the ex-Falck area in Milan, a children's hospice in Bologna, and residential buildings in Lisbon.

Giorgio Bianchi (Partner), born in 1957, studied architecture in Genoa. He joined RPBW (Genoa) in 1985. In 1995, he moved to RPBW Paris to work on the Stage Theater at Potsdamer Platz. A Partner since 1997, he was responsible for the rehabilitation of the Pompidou Center, Morgan Library expansion, and a private house in Colorado. He has worked on the design of all RPBW exhibitions since 2000. He is currently leading the team for the Stavros Niarchos Foundation Cultural Center in Athens and the Kum & Go headquarters in Des Moines.

Emanuela Baglietto (Partner), born in 1960, studied at the Genoa School of Architecture, and joined RPBW (Genoa) in 1988. She was lead architect for the Credito Industriale Sardo project. A Partner since 1997, she was responsible for the Mercedes-Benz Design Center, Nasher Sculpture Center, Isabella Stewart Gardner Museum, and Astrup Fearnley Museum. Recent projects include the design of the Centro Botín in Santander and a residential project in Sydney.

Collaborators

1971–77 ▶ Centre Georges Pompidou, Paris, France; *Client*: Ministry of Cultural Affairs, Ministry of National Education; Studio Piano & Rogers, architects

1996–2000 ▶ Refurbishment of the Centre Georges Pompidou, Paris, France; *Client*: Centre Georges Pompidou; RPBW, architects

1981–87 ▶ The Menil Collection, Houston, Texas, USA; *Client*: The Menil Foundation; Piano & Fitzgerald, architects

1985–2001 ▶ Redevelopment of the Old Harbor of Genoa, Genoa, Italy; *Client*: City of Genoa + Porto Antico SpA; RPBW, architects

1983–2003 ▶ Lingotto Factory Conversion, Turin, Italy; *Client*: Fiat S.p.A. (Competition, 1983); *Clients*: Lingotto S.p.A. + Pathé + Palazzo Grassi (Design Development and Construction phase, 1991–2003); RPBW, architects

2000–02 ▶ The Giovanni and Marella Agnelli Art Gallery at Lingotto, Turin, Italy; *Client*: Lingotto S.p.A. + Palazzo Grassi; RPBW, architects

1988–94 ▶ Kansai International Airport Terminal, Osaka, Japan; *Client*: Kansai International Airport Co. Ltd.; RPBW, architects; N. Okabe, senior partner in charge in association with Nikken Sekkei Ltd., Aéroports de Paris, Japan Airport Consultants Inc.

1989–91 ▶ Renzo Piano Building Workshop Punta Nave, Genoa, Italy; *Client*: Renzo Piano Building Workshop; RPBW, architects

1991–2001 ▶ Banca Popolare di Lodi, Lodi, Italy; *Client*: Banca Popolare di Lodi; RPBW, architects

1991–98 ▶ Jean-Marie Tjibaou Cultural Center, Nouméa, New Caledonia; *Client*: Agence pour le Développement de la Culture Kanak; RPBW, architects

1992–2000 ▶ Potsdamer Platz, Berlin, Germany; *Client*: Daimler-Chrysler AG; RPBW, architects; in association with Christoph Kohlbecker (Gaggenau)

1991–97 ▶ Beyeler Foundation Museum, Riehen (Basel), Switzerland; *Client*: Beyeler Foundation; RPBW, architects; in association with Burckhardt + Partner AG, Basel

1997–2001 ▶ Niccolò Paganini Auditorium, Parma, Italy; *Client*: City of Parma; RPBW, architects

1998–2001 ▶ Maison Hermès, Tokyo, Japan; *Client*: Hermès Japon; RPBW, architects; in collaboration with Rena Dumas Architecture Intérieure (Paris)

1994–2002 ▶ Parco della Musica Auditorium, Rome, Italy; *Client*: City of Rome; RPBW, architects

1996–2000 ▶ Aurora Place, office and residential buildings, Sydney, Australia; *Client*: Lend Lease Development; RPBW, architects; in collaboration with Lend Lease Design Group, Sydney (Schematic Design, 1996); in collaboration with Lend Lease Design Group and Group GSA Pty Ltd, Sydney (Design Development and Construction phase, 1997–2000)

1999–2003 ▶ Nasher Sculpture Center, Dallas, Texas, USA; *Client*: The Nasher Foundation; RPBW, architects

1999–2005 ▶ Zentrum Paul Klee, Bern, Switzerland; *Client*: Maurice E. and Martha Müller Foundation; RPBW, architects; in collaboration with ARB, architects (Bern)

1999–2005 ▶ High Museum of Art Expansion, Atlanta, Georgia, USA; *Client*: High Museum of Art + Woodruff Arts Center; RPBW, architects; in collaboration with Lord, Aeck & Sargent Inc., architects (Atlanta)

2000–06 ▶ Morgan Library Renovation and Expansion, New York, New York, USA; *Client*: The Morgan Library; RPBW, architects; in collaboration with Beyer Blinder Belle LLP (New York)

2000–07 ▶ The New York Times Building, New York, New York, USA; *Client*: The New York Times / Forest City Ratner Companies; RPBW, architects; in collaboration with FXFowle Architects, P.C. (New York)

2000–08 ▶ California Academy of Sciences Renovation and Expansion, San Francisco, California, USA; *Client*: California Academy of Sciences; RPBW, architects; in collaboration with Stantec Architecture (San Francisco)

2000–09 ▶ Modern Wing of the Art Institute of Chicago, Chicago, Illinois, USA; *Client*: The Art Institute of Chicago; RPBW, architects; in collaboration with Interactive Design Inc., architects (Chicago)

2002–10 ▶ Central Saint Giles Mixed-Use Development, London, UK; *Client*: Legal & General with Mitsubishi Estate Corporation Stanhope PLC; RPBW, architects; in collaboration with Fletcher Priest Architects (London)

2003–08 ▶ Broad Contemporary Art Museum (LACMA Expansion – Phase I), Los Angeles, California, USA; *Client*: Los Angeles County Museum of Art (LACMA); RPBW, architects; in collaboration with Gensler Associates (Santa Monica)

2006–10 ▶ The Resnick Pavilion (LACMA Expansion – Phase II), Los Angeles, California, USA; *Client*: Los Angeles County Museum of Art (LACMA); RPBW, architects; in collaboration with Gensler Associates (Santa Monica)

2000–12 ▶ The Shard – London Bridge Tower, London, UK; *Client*: Sellar Property Group; RPBW, architects; in collaboration with Adamson Associates (Toronto, London)

2006–12 ▶ Astrup Fearnley Museum of Modern Art, Oslo, Norway; *Client*: Selvaag Gruppen / Aspelin Ramm Gruppen; RPBW, architects; in collaboration with Narud Stokke Wiig (Oslo)

2010–12 ▶ Auditorium del Parco, L'Aquila, Italy; *Client*: Provincia Autonoma di Trento; RPBW, architects; in collaboration with Atelier Traldi, Milan

2007–13 ▶ Kimbell Art Museum Expansion, Fort Worth, Texas, USA; *Client*: Kimbell Art Foundation; RPBW, architects; in collaboration with Kendall/Heaton Associates, Inc. (Houston)

2007–15 ▶ The Whitney Museum of American Art, New York, New York, USA; *Client*: Whitney Museum of American Art; RPBW, architects; in collaboration with Cooper Robertson (New York)

World Map

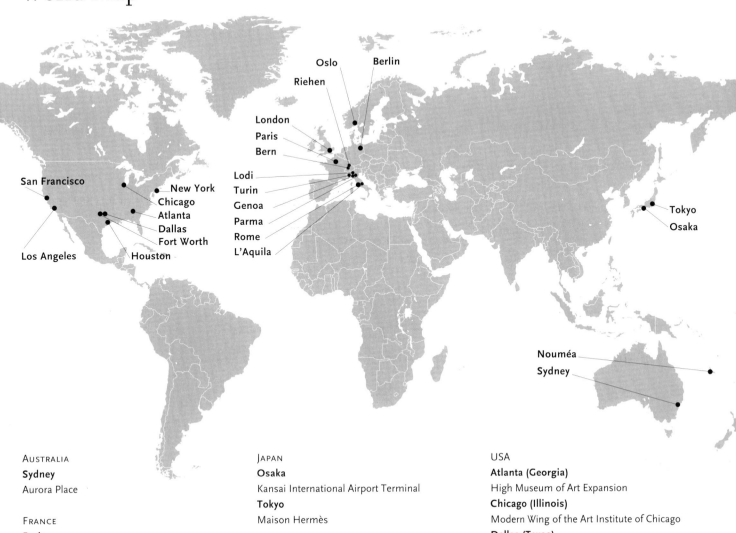

Oslo
Berlin
Riehen
London
Paris
Bern
Lodi
Turin
Genoa
Parma
Rome
L'Aquila

San Francisco
New York
Chicago
Atlanta
Dallas
Fort Worth
Los Angeles
Houston

Tokyo
Osaka

Nouméa
Sydney

AUSTRALIA
Sydney
Aurora Place

FRANCE
Paris
Centre Georges Pompidou

GERMANY
Berlin
Potsdamer Platz Reconstruction

ITALY
Genoa
Redevelopment of the Old Harbor of Genoa
Renzo Piano Building Workshop
L'Aquila
Auditorium del Parco
Lodi
Banca Popolare di Lodi
Parma
Niccolò Paganini Auditorium
Rome
Parco della Musica Auditorium
Turin
Lingotto Factory Conversion

JAPAN
Osaka
Kansai International Airport Terminal
Tokyo
Maison Hermès

NEW CALEDONIA
Nouméa
Jean-Marie Tjibaou Cultural Center

NORWAY
Oslo
Astrup Fearnley Museum of Modern Art

SWITZERLAND
Bern
Zentrum Paul Klee
Riehen (Basel)
Beyeler Foundation

UK
London
Central Saint Giles Mixed-Use Development
The Shard – London Bridge Tower

USA
Atlanta (Georgia)
High Museum of Art Expansion
Chicago (Illinois)
Modern Wing of the Art Institute of Chicago
Dallas (Texas)
Nasher Sculpture Center
Fort Worth (Texas)
Kimbell Art Museum Expansion
Houston (Texas)
Menil Collection
Los Angeles (California)
Los Angeles County Museum of Art (BCAM
  and the Resnick Pavilion)
New York (New York)
Morgan Library Renovation and Expansion
The New York Times Building
The Whitney Museum of American Art
San Francisco (California)
California Academy of Sciences Renovation
  and Expansion

Main Prizes

Main Bibliography

M. Dini: *Renzo Piano. Progetti e architetture 1964–1983*, Electa, Milan, Italy, 1983

R. Piano: *Progetti e Architetture 1984–1986*, Electa, Milan, Italy, 1986

R. Piano: *Renzo Piano*, Editions du Centre Pompidou, Paris, France, 1987

R. Piano: *Renzo Piano Buildings and Projects 1971–1989*, Rizzoli International, New York, USA, 1989

R. Piano: *Renzo Piano Building Workshop 1964–1991, In Search of a Balance*, Process architecture, Tokyo, Japan, n. 100, 1992

P. Buchanan: *Renzo Piano Building Workshop. Complete Works*, Vol. 1–5, Phaidon Press, London, UK, 1993/1995/1997/2000/2008

R. Piano: *Giornale di bordo*, Passigli ed., Florence, Italy, 1997, re-edition 2005

K. Frampton: *Renzo Piano Building Workshop*, GA Architect, n° 14, A.D.A. Edita Tokyo, Tokyo, Japan, 1997

A. Cuito: *Renzo Piano*, Loft Publications, Barcelona, Spain, 2002

E. Pizzi: *Renzo Piano*, Birkhäuser, Switzerland, 2002

R. Piano: *On Tour with Renzo Piano*, Phaidon Press, London, UK, 2004

P. Jodidio: *Piano. Renzo Piano Building Workshop 1966–2005*; Taschen, Cologne, Germany, 2005

R. Cassigoli: *La responsabilità dell'architetto*, Passigli ed., Florence, Italy, 2007 – re-edition

R. Piano, Olivier Favier: *La désobéissance de l'architecte*, Arléa ed., Paris, France, 2007

R. Piano: *Renzo Piano Building Workshop 1990–2006*, AV Monografias (Arquitectura Viva) n° 119, May–June 2006

V. Newhouse: *Renzo Piano Museums*, Monacelli Press, New York, USA, 2007

C. Conforti, F. Dal Co: *Renzo Piano gli schizzi*, Electa, Milan, Italy, 2007

R. Piano: *The Menil Collection*, Monograph, Renzo Piano Foundation, 2007

R. Piano: *Fondation Beyeler*, Monograph, Renzo Piano Foundation, 2008

R. Piano: *Nouméa Centre Culturel Jean-Marie Tjibaou*, Renzo Piano Foundation, 2009

A+U: *Renzo Piano Building Workshop 1989–2010*, Tokyo, 2010

R. Piano: *San Francisco California Academy of Sciences*, Renzo Piano Foundation, 2010

P. Jodidio: *Piano*, Taschen, Cologne, 2012

R. Piano: *The Shard*, Monograph, Renzo Piano Foundation, 2013

P. Jodidio: *Piano. Renzo Piano Building Workshop 1966–2014*, Taschen, Cologne, 2014

R. Piano: *Ronchamp*, Monograph, Renzo Piano Foundation, 2014

R. Piano: *Whitney*, Monograph, Renzo Piano Foundation, 2015

Credits